MYSTERIOUS ❖ DEATHS

John F. Kennedy

by David Pietrusza

Lucent Books
P.O. Box 289011, San Diego, CA 92198-9011

These titles are included in the *Mysterious Deaths* series:

Butch Cassidy   The Little Princes in the Tower
Amelia Earhart   Malcolm X
John F. Kennedy   Marilyn Monroe
Abraham Lincoln   Mozart

Cover design: Carl Franzen

Library of Congress Cataloging-in-Publication Data

Pietrusza, David, 1949–
    John F. Kennedy / by David Pietrusza.
        p.   cm. — (Mysterious deaths)
    Includes bibliographical references (p.   ) and index.
    Summary: Examines the unanswered questions surrounding circum-
stances of President Kennedy's assassination.
    ISBN 1-56006-263-0 (alk. paper)
    1. Kennedy, John F. (John Fitzgerald), 1917–1963—Assassination—
Juvenile literature. [1. Kennedy, John F. (John Fitzgerald), 1917–1963—
Assassination.] I. Title. II. Series.
E842.9.P5   1997
973.922—dc20   96-21510
                                                            CIP
                                                            AC

Printed in the U.S.A.
Copyright © 1997 by Lucent Books, Inc.
P.O. Box 289011, San Diego, CA 92198-9011

Contents

Haunting Human History

The *Mysterious Deaths* series focuses on nine individuals whose deaths have never been fully explained. Some are figures from the distant past; others are far more contemporary. Yet all of them remain fascinating as much for who they were and how they lived as for how they died. Their lives were characterized by fame and fortune, tragedy and triumph, secrets that led to acute vulnerability. Our enduring fascination with these stories, then, is due in part to the lives of the victims and in part to the array of conflicting facts and opinions, as well as the suspense, that surrounds their deaths.

Some of the people profiled in the *Mysterious Deaths* series were controversial political figures who lived and died in the public eye. John F. Kennedy, Abraham Lincoln, and Malcolm X were all killed in front of crowds as guards paid to protect them were unable to stop their murders. Despite all precautions, their assassins found ample opportunity to carry out their crimes. In each case, the assassins were tried and convicted. So what remains mysterious? As the reader will discover, everything.

The two women in the series, Marilyn Monroe and Amelia Earhart, are equally well remembered. Both died at the heights of their careers; both, from all appearances, had everything to live for. Yet their deaths have also been shrouded in mystery. While there are simple explanations—Monroe committed suicide, Earhart's plane crashed—the public has never been able to accept them. The more researchers dig into the deaths, the more mysterious evidence they unearth. Monroe's predilection for affairs with prominent politicians may have led to her death. Earhart, brash and cavalier, may have been involved in a government plot that collapsed around her. And these theories do not exhaust the mysterious possibilities that continue to puzzle researchers.

The circumstances of the deaths of the remaining figures in the *Mysterious Deaths* series—Richard III's nephews Edward and

4

Richard; the brilliant composer Wolfgang Mozart; and the infamous bank robber Butch Cassidy—are less well known but no less fascinating.

For example, what are almost surely the skeletons of the little princes Edward and Richard were found buried at the foot of a stairway in the Tower of London in 1674. To many, the discovery proved beyond a doubt that their evil uncle, Richard III, murdered them to attain the throne. Yet others find Richard wrongly accused, the obvious scapegoat. The mysterious tale of their deaths—full of dungeons, plots, and treachery—is still intriguing today.

In the history books, Wolfgang Mozart died in poverty from a consumptive-like disease. Yet there are reports and rumors, snatches of information culled from distant records, that Mozart may have died from a slow poisoning. Who could have wanted to murder the famous composer? And why?

Finally, bank robber Butch Cassidy's death couldn't have been less mysterious—shot to death by military police in Bolivia along with his companion, the Sundance Kid. Then why did members of Butch Cassidy's family and numerous others swear to have seen him, in full health, in the United States years after his supposed death?

These true-life whodunits are filled with tantalizing "what ifs?" What if Kennedy had used the bulletproof plastic hood that his Secret Servicemen had ready? What if Lincoln had decided not to attend the theater—which he did only to please his wife? What if Monroe's friend, Peter Lawford, receiving no answer to his persistent calls, had gone to her house, as he wanted to do? These questions frustrate us as well as testify to a haunting aspect of human history—the way that seemingly insignificant decisions can alter its course.

A Popular President

Despite his brief tenure in the White House, President John Fitzgerald Kennedy remains one of America's most fondly remembered and admired presidents.

Born to a politically active Irish Catholic family (his maternal grandfather was mayor of Boston), Kennedy was groomed for leadership. Originally, his older brother, Joe, was expected to lead the family to the White House, but when Joe was killed in World War II, "Jack" Kennedy took his place as the Kennedy most likely to be president. Jack was educated at Harvard and became a wartime hero when he not only survived the wreck of his PT boat in the Pacific, but also rescued other crewmen. In 1946 he was elected to the House of Representatives and in 1952 to the U.S. Senate. In 1956 he made an unsuccessful bid for the Democratic vice presidential nomination.

In 1960 the 43-year-old Kennedy sought a far greater prize: the presidency. His bid caused controversy, for if elected he would be the first Roman Catholic president, and many non-Catholics feared that a Catholic in the White House would take orders from the pope in Rome. Kennedy overcame such bigotry and that November won a paper-thin victory over Vice President Richard M. Nixon.

Kennedy's presidency was compared to the legendary realm of King Arthur, called Camelot. The handsome young president and his beautiful wife, Jacqueline Bouvier Kennedy, brought glamour to Washington. They appreciated the arts and were avid readers (Jack had even won a Pulitzer Prize for writing *Profiles in Courage*). Kennedy's call for sacrifice and patriotism inspired many Americans. "Ask not what your country can do for you," he told listeners at his inauguration, "ask what you can do for your country." To further his goals he founded the Peace Corps and boldly proposed putting a man on the moon. He asked for such things, he told audiences, "not because they are easy but because they are hard."

The Kennedy years were also years of turmoil. Many of the conflicts that Kennedy faced would become a part of the various conspiracy theories that circulated after his assassination. Among the problems that dogged his presidency were racial integration, organized crime, and the cold war. Protests erupted throughout the South as black Americans fought to break down the barriers of decades of segregation. Kennedy responded by ordering troops to help integrate the University of Alabama and by pushing civil rights legislation in the Congress. Many white southerners still favored segregation and greatly resented Kennedy's efforts.

Although John F. Kennedy's tenure in the White House was brief, he remains one of the most fondly remembered presidents of our time.

The president's brother, Attorney General Robert F. Kennedy, took bold steps against mob leaders, including International Brotherhood of Teamsters leader Jimmy Hoffa. Racketeers felt betrayed by the Kennedy brothers and shed no tears over either brother's death.

Tensions were high abroad, with the threat of nuclear destruction always possible as American and Soviet interests clashed around the world. In Germany, Soviet leader Nikita Khrushchev challenged Kennedy by building the Berlin Wall, which sealed off the Western enclave of West Berlin. In Southeast Asia communist insurgencies threatened Laos and South Vietnam. Kennedy responded by sending an ever-increasing number of so-called advisers, who actually provided military assistance to local governments.

The continuing presence of pro-Soviet dictator Fidel Castro in Cuba was particularly troublesome. In 1960 Kennedy criticized the

JFK was inaugurated in 1960 and led the country during one of the most tumultuous times in U.S. history.

President Kennedy negotiated one of the most frightening struggles for power in U.S. history during the Cuban Missile Crisis. Fidel Castro (pictured) allowed Soviet leaders to place nuclear missile silos in Cuba touching off an international crisis.

Eisenhower administration for not doing enough to topple Castro. The following year a U.S.-backed invasion of Cuba, the Bay of Pigs invasion, failed miserably; the episode was a great embarrassment to Kennedy. In 1962 the Soviets began placing nuclear missiles in Cuba. Never before had Soviet warheads been so near American cities. JFK responded by blockading Cuba and turning back Soviet ships; he threatened to escalate the conflict if Khrushchev did not pull the missiles out. No one knew how the Soviet leader would respond. Would he refuse to compromise and risk a nuclear confrontation? The Soviet ships finally turned back, and an agreement was reached. The Soviets promised to pull their missiles out of the Caribbean island, but many anticommunist Americans (and most Cuban exiles living in this country) feared that Kennedy had promised to leave the widely hated Castro dictatorship in place as part of the deal. Later, some conspiracy theorists would see these anti-Castro groups as prime suspects in Kennedy's death; other theorists implicated Castro himself.

In late 1963 Kennedy's political future was by no means assured, and he scheduled a visit to Texas to help shore up support in that key state.

CHAPTER

1

"They Are Going to Kill Us All!"

To a politician every season is a political season, and President John F. Kennedy was no exception. Especially now that he was less than a year away from the next presidential election.

In late November 1963, Kennedy knew that his reelection in 1964 was hardly secure. Winning the state of Texas was crucial to Kennedy's reelection campaign: No Democrat had ever won a presidential election without carrying Texas. Even with Texan Lyndon Baines Johnson on the ticket, Kennedy's popularity was dwindling in the conservative state.

So President Kennedy was going to Texas.

President Kennedy arrives in Fort Worth, Texas, in 1963 to the smiling faces of crowds of supporters.

John and Jacqueline Kennedy arrive in Dallas, Texas. It would prove to be the start of a tragic day for Jacqueline and the rest of the nation.

The Trip

Kennedy's Texas itinerary included appearances in San Antonio, Houston, Fort Worth, Dallas, and the capital city of Austin. He would be in the state for three days, from Thursday, November 21, until Saturday, November 23.

Complicating the visit was the bitter rivalry between Texas governor John Connally, a conservative Democrat and Johnson's longtime ally, and Texas senator Ralph Yarborough, a more liberal member of the president's party. They detested each other, and the two bickered childishly over who would ride in which car and who would be invited to which functions. At one point Kennedy forcefully told Yarborough he would either ride in the same car as Lyndon Johnson or walk.

Also traveling with JFK was his popular wife, Jacqueline. Although she was clearly a campaign asset, she had never previously accompanied her husband on a political trip. Her presence was so important that the president took the time to help her choose her wardrobe. They selected a pink wool suit with a navy blue collar and a matching pink pillbox hat. Jackie did not usually wear hats, but she would be riding in several motorcades, and a hat was necessary to keep her hairdo from being spoiled by the wind. "If it's so important that I look all right in Dallas," she complained to her husband, "why do I have to be blown around in a motorcade first?"

"Wanted for Treason"

The Kennedy team did not look forward to visiting Dallas. It was one of the more Republican and conservative cities in the state, and even its Democrats were far more conservative than the president and the majority of his party were. In addition, disturbing events were happening in the city.

On April 10, 1963, General Edwin Walker, an unsuccessful right-wing Texas gubernatorial candidate who had been removed from his army command in Europe for giving highly political lectures to his troops, was the target of an assassination attempt. He had narrowly missed death while sitting in his own dining room. A window frame deflected the well-aimed bullet and saved his life. It was such a close call that the bullet passed through Walker's hair instead of through his skull. Even though Walker was a political op-

A few months before Kennedy arrived in Dallas, an assassination attempt had been made on General Edwin Walker (pictured) while he was at home.

ponent of Kennedy, the fact that an assassin had targeted a public figure was alarming to Kennedy's staff.

There were other ominous incidents—some aimed at more liberal figures. That October on United Nations Day, UN ambassador Adlai E. Stevenson had visited Dallas. A crowd of noisy, jeering protesters jostled him and even spat on him. One woman hit his head with a placard. Other Dallasites were embarrassed by the incident, and Dallas mayor Earle Cabell said the city could make up for the display of hostility by giving Kennedy a warm welcome.

Yet as the visit drew closer there were growing signals that Kennedy would not receive a warm welcome. On November 21, 1963, someone distributed five thousand inflammatory handbills on city streets. They featured the president's picture and read "Wanted for Treason"; they were meant to criticize Kennedy for not being tough enough on Castro and communism. On the day of the visit, the American Fact Finding Committee ran a full-page ad in the *Dallas Morning News*. Trimmed with a quarter-inch-wide black border, it was less fiery than the handbill, but still accused the president of being "soft on Communists" and persecuting "loyal Americans."

It was no wonder that Kennedy's advisers did not relish visiting Dallas in what others would later describe as an "atmosphere of hate."

The Motorcade

Yet as Kennedy awoke on the morning of Friday, November 22, he had reason to be optimistic. Large and enthusiastic crowds greeted him at San Antonio and Houston, and the response had been the same at Fort Worth. It looked as if JFK might carry Texas in 1964 after all.

That morning the presidential party flew from Fort Worth to Dallas. The cities are virtually next to each other, and the flight took only thirteen minutes. Just before boarding the plane Kennedy spoke almost casually to his special assistant Kenneth O'Donnell about the possibility of assassination. "All one had to do," said JFK, "was get on a high building someday with a telescopic rifle, and there was nothing anybody could do."

At 11:40 A.M. *Air Force One*, the presidential aircraft, landed at Dallas's Love Field. A few minutes later the presidential motorcade left for downtown Dallas.

WANTED

FOR

TREASON

THIS MAN is wanted for treasonous

THIS MAN is wanted for treasonous

THIS MAN is wanted for treasonous activities against the United States:

1. Betraying the Constitution (which he swore to uphold):
He is turning the sovereignty of the U. S. over to the communist controlled United Nations.
He is betraying our friends (Cuba, Katanga, Portugal) and befriending our enemies (Russia, Yugoslavia, Poland).

2. He has been **WRONG** on innumerable issues affecting the security of the U.S. (United Nations-Berlin wall-Missle removal-Cuba-Wheat deals-Test Ban Treaty,etc.)

3. He has been lax in enforcing Communist Registration laws.

4. He has given support and encouragement to the Communist inspired racial riots.

5. He has illegally invaded a sovereign State with federal troops.

6. He has consistantly appointed Anti-Christians to Federal office: Upholds the Supreme Court in its Anti-Christian rulings.
Aliens and known Communists abound in Federal offices.

7. He has been caught in fantastic LIES to the American people (including personal ones like his previous marrage and divorce).

One of the "treason" handbills distributed in Dallas before Kennedy's assassination. Many people believed Kennedy had not taken a tough enough stand against communism.

Two Dallas police motorcycles led the way. Police Chief Jesse Curry drove the lead car, a white Ford, and Winston G. Lawson, the Secret Service's advance agent for the trip, accompanied him. Three more motorcycle police followed. Then came the midnight blue presidential limousine, an oversized Lincoln, officially dubbed SS 100 X. Two Secret Service agents, Roy Kellerman and Bill Greer, rode in the front seat with Governor and Mrs. Connally riding directly in back of them. The Kennedys were behind the Connallys, with John Kennedy on the right and Jacqueline

Kennedy on the left. A bouquet of red roses was on the seat between the Kennedys. On each side of the car and slightly behind it (a breach of security policy) rode two more motorcycle police. To avoid blocking the public's view they were ordered not to pull up even with the presidential limousine unless there was trouble.

Two other simple security precautions were violated that day. Each side of the car had been designed to hold a standing Secret Service agent, but because these men would partially block the public's view of the president, Kennedy ordered them not to take their security positions. The car also featured a plastic bubbletop for protection against rain. Most people thought it was bulletproof. It wasn't, but it might have slightly deflected the path of any bullet aimed at the car. Because the temperature had reached the seventies, Kenny O'Donnell ordered the Secret Service not to mount it in place.

Immediately following the presidential vehicle was a 1956 Cadillac convertible carrying O'Donnell, fellow presidential aide Dave Powers, and eight more Secret Service agents. Each agent was armed with a .38-caliber pistol. Between agents George Hickey and Glen Barrett was a powerful AR-15 automatic rifle.

Kennedy rides in the presidential limousine with Jackie and Texas governor John Connally (in foreground) before being fatally shot.

"They Just Can't Protect That Much"

Every American president lives with danger. Three other American presidents, Abraham Lincoln, James Garfield, and William McKinley, died from assassins' bullets. Within John Kennedy's lifetime, two chief executives, Franklin Roosevelt and Harry Truman, had been targets of unsuccessful assassination attempts.

Kennedy was a keen student of history and knew these facts. Occasionally he would joke about the possibility of assassination. Once while leaving church, he whispered to the two Secret Service agents ahead of him, "If there is anybody in that choir loft trying to get me, they're going to get you first."

Another time when Kennedy was riding in a car in California, an admirer tossed a tiny life jacket in the vehicle as a reminder of the president's naval experiences in World War II. It landed right between the president and his aide, Dave Powers. It was a life jacket, but it *could* have been a bomb. Again Kennedy joked. "If anyone wanted to kill you, you wouldn't be around," he told his assistant.

Kennedy had read Jim Bishop's book *The Day Lincoln Was Shot*, and casually remarked to the author, "My feelings about assassination are identical with Mr. Lincoln's. Anyone who wants to exchange his life for mine can take it." Then he added, "They just can't protect that much."

Next in the motorcade was the rented Lincoln convertible that carried Vice President Lyndon Johnson and Senator Yarborough. While Yarborough waved frantically to the crowds, Johnson looked unhappy to be sharing a ride with his more liberal Texas rival.

Dealey Plaza

Kennedy's destination was the Dallas Trade Mart, where he would speak at a luncheon before twenty-five hundred people. From Love Field the motorcade traveled in a straight line down Main Street, but it needed to make one sharp turn at Dealey Plaza.

Dealey Plaza was an oddly shaped, sloping park, dotted by reflecting fountains, some bleachers, and a statue of George Bannerman Dealey, a former publisher of the *Dallas Morning News*, the same paper that had run the controversial American Fact Finding Committee ad. The plaza was bounded on the east by Main Street, on the south by Commerce Street, on the north by Elm Street, and on the west by a railroad overpass (sometimes called the triple underpass because Elm, Main, and Commerce Streets passed under it).

The motorcade was scheduled to leave Main Street, turn left at Houston Street, and head north along Dealey Plaza for just one block. Then it would make a sharp left turn onto Elm Street, a 120-degree arc. Kennedy's limousine would be going approximately eleven miles per hour—slow enough to be an inviting target.

On the northwest corner of Houston and Elm stood a seven-story, tan brick building built in 1901 and recently converted to a warehouse—the Texas School Book Depository. A number of depository employees gathered at the building's entrance in order to see the president and first lady close up. From the fifth floor's southeast corner three young, black employees peered down at

The Texas School Book Depository on Elm Street in Dallas where Lee Harvey Oswald waited for the presidential limousine to pass.

the scene below. From the street some spectators thought they saw a figure on the sixth floor. A fifteen-year-old schoolboy believed he saw a metal pipe sticking out a window, but didn't think it was important. Another spectator even thought the man on the sixth floor had a rifle but assumed he was there to protect the president.

Atop the depository's roof was a Hertz rent-a-car billboard with a huge clock. As the president's car turned onto Elm Street the clock read 12:30.

Just west of the depository building was a portion of Dealey Plaza that would become known as the grassy knoll. To the north of Elm Street was a slight hill. Atop the hill was a pergola, an open, colonnaded structure, and just west of the pergola was a five-foot-

Big John

Who was the man who sat in front of John Kennedy, who would share the pain of an assassin's bullet?

"Big John" Connally had long been a political ally of Kennedy's vice president, fellow Texan Lyndon Baines Johnson. In 1948 Connally masterminded Johnson's election to the U.S. Senate. Johnson's eighty-seven-vote victory margin earned him the nickname "Landslide Lyndon" and started widespread rumors of vote fraud.

At the beginning of John Kennedy's presidency Connally briefly served as secretary of the navy but returned to Texas to win election to the governorship. One of the candidates he defeated was General Edwin Walker.

Connally, a political conservative, later left the Democratic Party and became secretary of the treasury under President Richard Nixon. Some say Nixon saw him as his successor in the presidency, but this was not to be. Misfortune dogged Connally. He ran for the Republican nomination for president three times, and failed miserably each time. In 1974 he was indicted on charges of accepting a $10,000 bribe but was acquitted. In 1987 Connally's real estate holdings collapsed, and he was forced into bankruptcy. Connally had to sell virtually everything he owned to pay his debts.

When he died in June 1993, a small fragment of the bullet that struck him on November 22, 1963, was still imbedded in his body.

President Kennedy, Texas governor John Connally, and Jackie Kennedy ride through Dallas moments before Kennedy's assassination on November 22, 1963.

high picket fence. Beyond the fence was a parking lot for the Sheriff's Department employees. Across the street, on Elm Street's south side, stood a man carrying a black umbrella. As the president's car turned onto Elm, the man raised the umbrella over his head and opened it. Then he closed his umbrella, lowered it, and sat down on the curb.

"You Can't Say That Dallas Doesn't Love You"

The day was warmer than expected, and Jackie Kennedy in her pink wool suit was growing increasingly hot and uncomfortable. "We could see a tunnel in front of us," she later recalled. "Everything was really slow then. And I remember thinking it would be so cool under that tunnel."

It was quiet in the presidential car as the motorcade reached Elm Street, and the Kennedys and the Connallys were busy waving to the enthusiastic crowd. Mrs. Connally then looked over her shoulder toward the president, smiled, and said, "Mr. Kennedy, you can't say that Dallas doesn't love you."

"No, you certainly can't," JFK responded.

Secret Service agent Lawson, a former army counterintelligence officer, looked at his watch. It read 12:30. He picked up the limousine's microphone and called ahead to the Trade Mart, "We'll be there in about five minutes."

Just then a loud noise cracked through Dealey Plaza, and a flock of pigeons roosting atop the School Book Depository launched into panic-stricken flight. Some observers thought the sound was a car backfiring; others thought it a firecracker; but John Connally instinctively *knew* it was a rifle shot. On the fifth floor of the School Book Depository, the three workers heard the shots explode like thunder above their heads. They could even hear the click-click of a rifle bolt and the sound of spent cartridges hitting the plywood floor. One of them, Hank Norman, shouted, "It's coming right over our heads!"

An assassin's bullet whizzed past the presidential vehicle. It struck a curb, and the concrete it set loose whizzed by the president's face, probably nicking him. Agent Kellerman thought he heard the president say, "My God I am hit." Another fragment of

A spectator's camera captures the moment when the bullet from an assassin's rifle strikes Kennedy in the head, forcing him to slump lifelessly against his wife. Governor John Connally of Texas, who was also wounded, begins to turn around just to the left of Mrs. Kennedy.

Panicking, Jackie Kennedy tries to crawl out of the presidential limousine as secret service agent Clint Hill climbs toward her to push her back in the seat.

pavement sailed across Dealey Plaza all the way to Commerce Street where it struck spectator James Tague in the cheek. Blood began trickling down his face. Then there was a second shot. This one did not miss. It ripped through the president's back and out his throat. The president threw his arms up in response. Mrs. Kennedy saw her husband react to the shot and screamed: "What are they doing to you?"

Governor Connally was also hit, and his wife pulled him down into her lap. "Oh, no, no, no," moaned Connally, who had suffered multiple wounds. "They are going to kill us all."

Then Connally became still, and his wife thought he was dead. He moved just a little, and she comforted him, "It's all right. Be still."

In Vice President Johnson's convertible Secret Service agent Rufus Youngblood shoved the vice president out of the way and threw himself over his body to protect him, but in the presidential limousine the Secret Service was slow to react. Agent Greer, driving the president's car, knew something was wrong but didn't know what. Instead of accelerating, he slowed down, almost bringing the

Aboard Air Force One, Jackie Kennedy watches Lyndon B. Johnson as he is sworn in as president of the United States.

car to a halt so he could look back at the president. As he turned, another shot rang out.

The Connallys felt something splatter over the car. The president had been hit in the skull, and his brains had spewed out. A nearly hysterical Jacqueline Kennedy began crawling out the back of the car, over its trunk. Secret Service agent Clint Hill, who had been stationed in the backup car, ran forward and pushed her back into the seat. Bill Greer by now had finally responded properly and pushed his foot down on the accelerator.

"Pull out of the motorcade," roared Agent Roy Kellerman. "Take us to the nearest hospital."

Death Comes to the President

Their destination was Parkland Memorial Hospital where doctors battled to save Kennedy's and Connally's lives. Connally, despite multiple wounds, would live. But Kennedy never had a chance. From the second the bullet entered his skull, he was virtually dead. Nonetheless, Parkland's physicians, startled to suddenly find themselves treating the president of the United States, did all they could, including an emergency tracheotomy. They performed the

A Nation's Grief

The murder of their youthful president shocked Americans. Lyndon Johnson proclaimed the day of Kennedy's funeral, Monday, November 25, "to be a day of national mourning throughout the United States." But no one needed to tell the American people to mourn. Schools and businesses closed, and Americans gathered around their televisions to watch the funeral on television and to sadly marvel at the brave dignity of Jacqueline Kennedy and her two young children, Caroline and John, as they struggled with their sorrow. Millions wept openly as they watched three-year-old John salute his fallen father. Hundreds of thousands of mourners thronged the streets of Washington to view the president's coffin as it passed by. Kennedy was buried at the Arlington National Cemetery just outside Washington, and his grave was marked by an eternal flame, symbolizing the martyred president's eternal ideals.

Cape Canaveral, the space-launch site in Florida, was renamed Cape Kennedy. In Washington, to honor the first family's commitment to culture and the arts, the National Center for the Performing Arts became the Kennedy Center.

Reaction was similar abroad. Over 220 foreign dignitaries including President Charles de Gaulle of France (whose birthday was November 22 and who had himself survived several assassination attempts) and UN secretary general U Thant attended the funeral. Nikita Khrushchev cabled President Johnson that Kennedy's death was "a hard blow to all people who cherish the cause of peace and Soviet-American cooperation."

Jackie Kennedy is flanked by JFK's brothers, Ted and Robert, at John's funeral. John Jr. salutes his fallen father.

correct medical procedure but in doing so destroyed crucial evidence as to the nature of his wounds.

But evidence didn't seem important at the moment when a man's life hung in the balance.

Out in the hallway a hospital engineer bumped into one of the stretchers that brought the wounded men in. A 6.5-millimeter bullet rolled out on the floor. Had it passed through Connally? or Kennedy? or both?

Lyndon Johnson determined to return immediately to Washington. No one knew whether there was a conspiracy at work or whether he and other high government officials were also targeted for death. No one knew if any foreign governments had been involved. If there were, it could mean war, even nuclear war. On *Air Force One*, a grieving Jacqueline Kennedy, still in her blood-stained pink suit, watched Johnson take the presidential oath of office. The coffin containing the remains of her husband was at the rear of the plane, and the nation was plunging into a period of great sorrow—and confusion.

"An Unknown White Male"

As the motorcade sped to Parkland Hospital, police at Dealey Plaza faced a scene of incredible chaos. Who had committed this horrible act? Was there only one person involved? Where had the shots come from? Was there a threat of further violence?

In the confusion at Dealey Plaza everyone seemed to have a different version of what had just occurred. Many witnesses had no clear idea of where the shots had come from. Dealey Plaza, an open stretch of land virtually surrounded by high buildings, has been described as a virtual echo chamber; its acoustic properties add to the chaos and confusion.

Newspaper cameramen keep their cameras on Kennedy's fleeing limousine as it speeds toward Parkland Hospital.

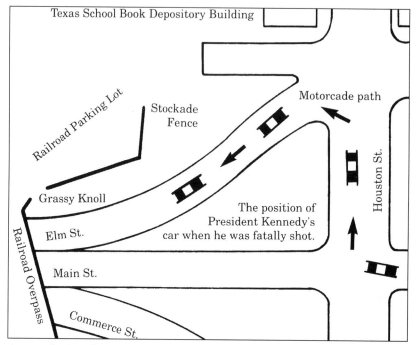

A map depicts the route Kennedy's limousine took. After the assassination, spectators had very different ideas about where the shots had come from.

Some thought the shots originated from the Texas School Book Depository just to the rear of the president's car. Others thought the shots came from behind the picket fence on the grassy knoll, more or less parallel to the vehicle. Some said they heard the shots from straight ahead, from the railroad overpass. One witness even claimed a shot had come inside the presidential limousine.

And how many shots had been fired? Almost nine out of ten witnesses believed there had been three, but some heard only two. A few even thought there had been four or more. One Secret Service agent described a "flurry of shells" hitting the presidential car.

A Dallas motorcycle policeman stopped his vehicle and ran up the grassy knoll. A portion of the crowd followed him. Were they fleeing to safety? Or were they heading towards the sound of the shooting?

Forty-five-year-old steamfitter Howard Brennan had been watching the motorcade on Houston Street. He was just 120 feet away from the School Book Depository's southeast sixth-floor corner. After the first shot roared out, he looked up towards the sixth floor where he had previously seen an individual he described as

The Zapruder Film

At Dealey Plaza, as well as all along the parade route, spectators filmed the presidential visit. At the plaza almost two dozen persons had cameras with them. Among them was Abraham Zapruder, an elderly dress manufacturer with offices in the Dal-Tex Building, across Houston Street from the Texas School Book Depository. Originally, Zapruder had left his eight-millimeter zoom-lens camera at home, but his secretary persuaded him to go back and retrieve it so he could record Kennedy's visit to Dealey Plaza for posterity. Now as the president rode past, Abraham Zapruder was perched on a four-foot-high embankment near the grassy knoll.

As the shooting began Zapruder resisted the temptation to panic or to swing around to where he thought the shots were coming from (in his case, he thought from behind the knoll). He kept filming the presidential limousine, providing the only full film of the assassination. The existence of the Zapruder film has enabled both critics and supporters of the official version of the assassination to argue their case by tying shots and events to a frame-by-frame study of the film.

Yet Zapruder was not the only motion picture photographer at Dealey Plaza. Marie Muchmore filmed the motorcade as it rolled onto Houston Street, and Orville Nix and Robert Hughes took movies from almost exactly opposite Zapruder on Main Street. Some observers thought Nix's film revealed a rifle barrel on the grassy knoll, although later analysis disputed that conclusion. Hughes shut off his camera just before the assassination. He turned it on again to record panic-stricken spectators fleeing toward the grassy knoll.

The Zapruder film shows John F. Kennedy after he was hit by the first bullet.

(Left) Witness Howard Brennan circled the areas where (a) he had seen a man firing at JFK, and (b) he had seen spectators watching the motorcade. (Right) A newsman stands in the spot where Oswald fired the shots that killed President Kennedy.

"unsmiling [but] calm." Now he saw that same man aiming a rifle at President Kennedy and squeezing off two more shots. "I wanted to cry, I wanted to scream," Brennan would later say, "but I couldn't utter a noise."

Brennan approached a policeman and told his story, providing the police with a description of the suspect. By now Dallas motorcycle police officer Marrion Baker was inside the School Book Depository. In the second floor lunchroom he came across a young man of medium height and weight. When told the man worked there, Baker let him walk out the front door.

At 12:45, just fifteen minutes after the assassination, a bulletin based on Howard Brennan's description went out on Dallas Police Department radios:

> Attention all squads—attention all squads. At Elm and Houston reported to be an unknown white male, approximately thirty, slender build, height five feet ten inches, 165 pounds—reported to be armed with what is believed to be a 30-caliber rifle . . . no further description or information at this time.

When police searched the building's sixth floor they came across a sniper's nest, surrounded by a wall of cartons. Hidden nearby was a bolt-action rifle, an Italian-made Mannlicher-Carcano. On the floor were three spent brass rifle shells. Inside the

Mannlicher-Carcano's chamber was a fourth, unfired bullet. Also found in the sniper's nest was an odd-sized paper bag, long enough to hold a rifle.

One School Book Depository employee, a $1.25-an-hour clerk named Lee Harvey Oswald, was mysteriously missing when management gathered the building's employees together. In fact, it was Oswald whom police officer Marrion Baker had discovered in the depository's cafeteria.

Oswald was under intense suspicion because he had been seen on the sixth floor that day, and he fit Howard Brennan's description of the assassin.

Officer Tippit

Dallas police officer J. D. Tippit must have heard Brennan's description on the radio. At 1:15 he saw Oswald hurrying along East Tenth Street in the city's Oak Cliff area. Tippit motioned for him to stop and then got out of his car. Oswald drew a Smith and Wesson .38-caliber revolver and fired several shots. Four hit Tippit: one in the forehead and one straight through the heart. He was dead when he hit the ground.

A half hour later a shoe store clerk saw Oswald on West Jefferson Boulevard. He acted suspiciously and then snuck into the Texas Theater without buying a ticket. As police surrounded their suspect in the darkened theater, the man pulled out a revolver, shouted "This is it," and tried to shoot another officer. Police grabbed the weapon and took twenty-four-year-old Lee Harvey Oswald into custody.

Officer Tippit

Later that afternoon, Dallas police visited the home of Oswald's estranged wife. (Oswald lived separately at a rooming house.) They told Marina Oswald that her husband had been arrested for shooting Officer Tippit and asked if he had any weapons. She said yes and went to the garage where he kept his Mannlicher-Carcano rifle in an old green and brown blanket. She picked up the blanket and was shocked to find that it was empty.

Lee Harvey Oswald immediately after his arrest. At first arrested for the death of Tippit, Oswald's behavior led officers to suspect he was also Kennedy's assassin.

Liar

At first Oswald was charged only with the murder of Officer Tippit, but as the hours passed the case against him grew. He denied owning a rifle, but that was a lie. Then police discovered he had ordered a Mannlicher-Carcano under the fictitious name of A. Hidell. He denied knowing anything about anyone named Hidell, but forgot he had a forged ID card in his wallet bearing the name Alek J. Hidell.

In their search of Oswald's wife's home, police discovered photographs of Oswald holding a rifle and a revolver. Oswald said that the pictures were fake—that the police had taken his picture after he was arrested and had superimposed his face on someone else's body. Marina admitted, though, that she had taken the pictures. Analysis would later prove the photos were genuine and, in fact, had been taken by Oswald's own camera.

He denied owning a pistol, but that too was a lie. He finally did admit owning one, but said he had purchased his pistol in Fort

Worth. Police confronted him with evidence that he ordered it from a firm in Los Angeles.

The evidence mounted. Fibers found on the assassination weapon matched those of the shirt Oswald was wearing when he was arrested. Oswald's fingerprints and palm prints matched those on the paper bag found on the sixth floor, and fibers on the bag matched those on the blanket at Marina Oswald's home. The man who had driven Oswald to work that morning said that Oswald claimed the package he was carrying into the depository contained curtain rods, but a package that size and shape could very well have contained a rifle.

One of the photos confiscated from Marina Oswald's home pictured Lee Harvey Oswald with the Mannlicher-Carcano rifle that he denied owning and that he used to shoot Kennedy.

The Most Famous Rifle in History

The weapon Dallas police found on the sixth floor of the Texas School Book Depository was a 6.5-millimeter Mannlicher-Carcano rifle, manufactured in Italy in 1940, serial number C2766.

The war-surplus rifle plus scope had been ordered from Chicago's Klein's Sporting Goods Company in March 1963 by A. Hidell, P.O. Box 2915, Dallas, Texas. That post office box had been rented by Lee Harvey Oswald. The order form and an accompanying postal money order for $21.45 were in Oswald's handwriting.

The rifle's cheap Japanese-made four-power (4X) telescopic sight was mounted slightly off center, but the Warren Commission contended that this error would have actually assisted the shooter in hitting a target moving away from him.

The Mannlicher-Carcano is a powerful weapon and has even been used to hunt elephants. Its muzzle speed was over two thousand feet per second, higher than any rifle used by the U.S. Army. Its bolt was difficult to operate, but Oswald was known to have spent hours practicing with it. The relatively low kickback of the Mannlicher-Carcano made accurate repeat firing easier.

Many assassination researchers have derided the quality of the Mannlicher-Carcano rifle. *Reasonable Doubt* author Henry Hurt quoted a *Mechanix Illustrated* product review that called the rifle "crudely-made, poorly designed, dangerous, inaccurate . . . unreliable on repeat shots." Robert Sam Anson said Italians had called it "the humanitarian rifle" because it rarely hit its targets. But the FBI found it to be "very accurate," and Jim Moore in *Conspiracy of One* contended it was a "reliable, accurate, and solid" weapon.

Oswald said he was having lunch in the cafeteria with another employee, Junior Jarman, when Kennedy was shot. Jarman was actually on the fifth floor when the shooting took place.

At 1:30 A.M. on Saturday, November 23, Lee Harvey Oswald was arraigned on the charge of murdering President John Fitzgerald Kennedy.

"I Dislike Everybody"

In the forty hours that followed the assassination, the American public learned that Lee Harvey Oswald was not a typical resident of Dallas. Oswald was born in New Orleans on October 18, 1939. His father had died two months before his birth. Oswald left the city at age four and returned briefly in 1950, when he stayed with his aunt Lillian Murret and her husband "Dutz" for two or three weeks. In the early 1950s he lived in New York City, where he developed a strong belief in communism and failed to fit in with his classmates.

At one point young Oswald told a school psychologist, "I dislike everybody." In November 1953 a judge ordered mandatory psychiatric care for the troubled teenager, but instead his mother took him back to New Orleans. While in high school in 1955 Lee was briefly a cadet with the local Civil Air Patrol (CAP); however, he dropped

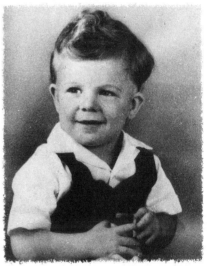

Lee Harvey Oswald, age 2

out of high school in eleventh grade. The family subsequently moved to Dallas, and in 1956 Oswald, following in an older brother's footsteps, enlisted in the U.S. Marine Corps. He qualified as a sharpshooter, one of the higher ratings given in shooting a rifle.

"I Have Had Enough"

In 1959 Oswald received an honorable discharge from the marines, claiming that his mother needed financial support. But instead of helping her, Oswald, just nineteen years old and still committed to Marxism, left for the Soviet Union.

Although the Soviets kept Oswald under some surveillance, they had little interest in encouraging him or other low-level, non-political defectors who had few U.S. secrets to reveal. The Soviets reasoned that life in the Soviet Union might not prove to be as interesting for Oswald as he may have believed from reading Soviet propaganda.

Marina and Lee Oswald depart Minsk for the United States. Although Oswald desperately wanted to renounce his American citizenship and move to the Soviet Union, once there he quickly grew bored and wanted to leave.

The Soviets refused him permission to live in their country, and it was only after officials found him in his hotel room with his wrists cut from a suicide attempt that they relented. In January 1960 Soviet officials told Oswald that they would allow him to live in Minsk, 450 miles southwest of Moscow, and that they had found a job for him as a metalworker in a local radio and television factory. He had his own one-room apartment, and, by Soviet standards, lived reasonably well.

But he soon grew unhappy in Minsk. He had hoped to attend a Soviet university, so factory employment was hardly his dream. Oswald quickly became bored with the job and grew increasingly dissatisfied with Soviet regimentation. "I have had enough," Oswald wrote in his diary. According to Norman Mailer in *Oswald's Tale*, "his behavior and attitude caused complaints from other workers." He was also unlucky in love. In January 1960 a young woman he described "as a silky, black haired Jewish beauty with fine dark eyes, skin as white as snow, [and] a beautiful smile" rejected his proposal of marriage.

The following month he decided to return to the United States, and the Soviet Union, which allowed others like him to leave, let him go. But before leaving, he met a young pharmacist named Marina Prusakova. Perhaps intrigued by the fact that he was an American, or by the fact that he had a private apartment, a rarity in Soviet life, she accepted his hasty proposal, tendered just one month after they met. Marina lived with her uncle, Ilya Vasilyvich Prusakova, a local lumber industry executive whose position also gave him the rank of colonel in the MVD, the Soviet Ministry of Internal Affairs, an organization that controlled the Soviet secret police and thus had links to espionage groups.

In June 1962 the Oswalds left the Soviet Union. Their next home would be with Oswald's brother in Fort Worth, Texas—just next door to Dallas—where Oswald supported himself with a series of low-paying menial jobs. His home life was also unhappy. Despite his high-sounding Marxist ideals, Oswald browbeat and abused his wife. "Absolute freedom for all was the core of his political vision," noted Norman Mailer in *Oswald's Tale*, "yet he treated Marina as if he were a Nazi corporal shaping up a recruit."

Hands Off Cuba!

In 1963 Oswald returned to New Orleans. In April 1963, just one week after the attempt on Edwin Walker's life, a now unemployed Oswald moved back to the city of his birth. He again lived with his aunt and uncle for a short period of time but soon went off on his own. He obtained a $1.50-an-hour job at the Reily Coffee Company and joined the Fair Play for Cuba Committee (FPCC). In fact, he was his chapter's only member. He defended pro-Castro activities to his skeptical wife, who thought he was wasting his time. "You laugh now," Oswald told her, "but in twenty years, when I'm prime minister [of the United States—an odd statement because the United States has no prime minister; perhaps he thought a communist government would create such a post], we'll see how you laugh then." He distributed FPCC handbills, stamping some of them with the address 544 Camp Street, a small office building located a block from the Reily Coffee Company that actually housed anticommunist organizations.

Strangely, in August 1963 Oswald told a group of anticommunist Cuban exiles that he also opposed the Castro regime. Shortly thereafter, they spotted him on the street, passing out his

Oswald distributes "Hands Off Cuba!" leaflets as part of his pro-Cuba efforts. Oswald had tried to gain entrance to Cuba, only to have the Cuban embassy reject him.

pro-Castro handbills. A scuffle ensued, and a local court fined Oswald ten dollars for disturbing the peace. Later he appeared on a local radio show, where he debated two anticommunists. During the debate the anticommunists began to personally attack Oswald. They had contacted the FBI and the House Un-American Activities Committee, which informed them of Oswald's discharge from the marines (which had been changed to "dishonorable" after it was discovered he obtained it under false pretenses) and defection to the Soviet Union. When they revealed this information on the air, Oswald, who had not expected these topics to surface, felt humiliated.

By now Oswald had been fired from the Reily Coffee Company. He had tried the Soviet Union and found it not to his liking. He was unemployed in the United States and thought the FBI was shadowing him and causing his problems. He determined to move to Cuba. In September 1963 Oswald left New Orleans for Mexico City, where he visited the Cuban embassy. But Cuban officials there refused to give him permission to enter Cuba. Discouraged and short on money, Oswald returned to Dallas. Marina Oswald and their two daughters continued to live with friends, and Oswald lived in a rooming house under the alias of O. H. Lee. On October 16, 1963, thanks to one of his wife's neighbors, he secured a new job—at the Texas School Book Depository.

The Patsy

Dallas police grilled Oswald for hours on end, but because under Texas law a defendant's spoken statements could not be used against him in court, the police neither tape-recorded the sessions (in 1963 the department did not even own a tape recorder) nor took notes. In any case, Oswald admitted nothing. He did request an attorney, but not a local one. Instead he demanded John Abt, a New Yorker well known for defending prominent members of the Communist Party.

The police were confident they had their man, but they wanted to know whether Oswald was part of some larger conspiracy, particularly in view of his procommunist background. Assistant District Attorney Bill Alexander participated in the search of Oswald's

Oswald shows the press his manacled hands shortly after his arrest. Police questioned Oswald for hours, trying to determine if he was part of a larger communist conspiracy to murder the president.

rented room where police found what Alexander described as "that Communist propaganda." "I thought," Alexander later recalled, "we might have stumbled across something with international repercussions, a spy ring or something like that."

To reporters at police headquarters, Oswald called out, "I'm just a patsy." When his brother Robert visited him in jail, Oswald warned him "not to form any opinion on the so-called evidence." To investigators he maintained a cool, even arrogant, composure. "He was so smug in a way he dealt with the questions," said Alexander, "at times I had to walk out of the room."

Occasionally, reporters and the television-viewing public could catch a glimpse of the alleged assassin as he was led about the police department. The annoying smirk on his face probably diluted any sympathy viewers might have felt for the young man. New Orleans district attorney Jim Garrison watched Oswald on television and recalled, "You could feel the sudden explosion of fury, the outburst of hate against this previously unknown young man." Many Americans wanted to kill him. Soon one would.

"I Am Jack Ruby"

On Sunday morning, November 24, Oswald was to be transferred to the county jail. He would take an elevator from the third floor to the police department's basement; step out in a corridor past a horde of newspaper, television, and radio reporters; and walk down a ramp into a waiting armored truck.

At 11:21 Oswald, handcuffed to two police officers, walked into the corridor. "Here he comes!" someone shouted as the television floodlights flashed on. Millions of shocked television viewers witnessed what happened next. A heavyset middle-aged man in a dark brown suit and a snap-brim, gray felt hat burst through the crowd. In his hand was a Colt .38-caliber revolver, and as he surged forward he yelled, "You killed my president, you rat!"

The police saw him coming but could do nothing. One recognized him and called out: "Jack, you son of a bitch!" The attacker fired one shot at point-blank range into Oswald's stomach. Oswald fell to the ground, never able to say another word. In three minutes an ambulance arrived to speed him to a hospital—Parkland Memorial Hospital—where he died at 2:07 P.M.

The police wrestled the assailant to the ground. As they held him down, he said, "I am Jack Ruby. You all know me."

Jack Ruby (with gun) crosses in front of police officers to shoot Lee Harvey Oswald at point-blank range. Theories abound as to why Ruby shot Oswald.

"Someone Tore My Heart Out"

Many police officers *did* know Jack Ruby. So did many of the reporters in the crowded corridor. Born in Chicago in 1911, Ruby had lived in Dallas since 1947 where he operated a seedy nightclub called the Carousel Club. Many of his acquaintances in both Chicago and Dallas were connected to underworld activities. Jack Ruby was a flashy, showy character of barely average intelligence, emotionally unstable, and prone to violence. His business sense left much to be desired; in November 1963 he was heavily in debt and on the verge of financial ruin.

As Kennedy was being assassinated at Dealey Plaza, Ruby was only five blocks away at the offices of the *Dallas Morning News*, placing an ad for his club. Although he really couldn't afford to do so, the ad announced he was deciding to honor JFK by closing the Carousel Club for the weekend.

Those who saw Jack Ruby during the next forty-eight hours remembered a man profoundly troubled by Kennedy's death. He wept openly at the thought of the grieving Jacqueline Kennedy and her two small children. "I never felt so bad in my life," he cried to his sister Eva, "even when Ma and Pa died.... Someone tore my heart out."

The Jewish Ruby brooded over the thought that the "Welcome, Mr. President" ad in the November 22 *Morning News* and signed by a Bernard Weissman might be linked to Jews. Ruby was very sensitive to anything that might reflect badly on Jews and often answered perceived slights with his fists. Also bothering Ruby were the Impeach Earl Warren billboards he saw on Dallas streets. He

Ruby, flanked by showgirls, in front of his club. A Kennedy supporter, Ruby was terribly upset over JFK's assassination and the plight of Jackie and Kennedy's children.

wasn't sure who Earl Warren was, but he thought the messages might have something to do with the assassination and took some pictures of them over the weekend. (Earl Warren was the chief justice of the U.S. Supreme Court.)

But above all Ruby wanted to be where the action was. He *always* did. Although he denied it that weekend, he probably visited Parkland Hospital and Dealey Plaza. He showed up numerous times at police headquarters, sometimes bringing sandwiches to reporters, other times acting like a reporter himself. On Friday night Oswald stood just a few feet away from Ruby, who probably had a revolver in his jacket even then.

When Jack Ruby pulled the trigger on Sunday afternoon, he silenced Lee Harvey Oswald forever—and only increased the fever of speculation that a conspiracy was involved.

The Warren Report: Did Oswald Act Alone?

A week after the assassination a Gallup Poll revealed that only 29 percent of Americans believed that Oswald had acted alone. Oswald's procommunist sympathies encouraged the suspicion that either the Soviet Union or Cuba was somehow involved.

To help resolve the questions Americans had—and also to quiet their fears—President Lyndon Johnson appointed Chief Justice Earl Warren of the Supreme Court to lead a blue-ribbon commission (which would become known to history as the Warren Commission) to investigate Kennedy's assassination and report its

Members of the Warren Commission appointed by President Johnson to lead an investigation into JFK's death. From left to right, Allen Dulles, Hale Boggs, John Sherman Cooper, Earl Warren, Richard Russell, John McCloy, and Gerald Ford.

The Warren Commission hands President Johnson its report on the Kennedy assassination. The commission concluded that a conspiracy did not exist and that Oswald and Ruby had acted alone.

conclusions to the nation. Among its seven members were former CIA director Allen Dulles, Georgia senator Richard Russell, and Michigan representative Gerald Ford.

In September 1964 the commission issued its 888-page final report and twenty-six volumes of supporting evidence. The bottom line: "The Commission has found no evidence that either Lee Harvey Oswald or Jack Ruby was part of any conspiracy, domestic or foreign, to assassinate President Kennedy."

The Warren Commission uncovered a great deal of data that has not been questioned, including the fact that it was Oswald who had attempted to kill General Edwin Walker, a man Oswald thought was an extremist and a fascist. But the Warren Commission Report had many flaws, and these shortcomings would give rise to criticism of its work that continues to this day.

The commission did not use its own independent investigators to gather much of its evidence. Instead, it relied heavily on Secret Service and FBI agents for assistance. Both agencies had reason to downplay or hide material that might prove embarrassing. The FBI provided only information that commission staff members specifically requested. Even author Gerald Posner, who basically supported the Warren Commission's findings, admitted "the FBI did not treat the Commission as its partner in search of the truth." The CIA never informed the commission of its plots to kill Fidel Castro.

PHOTOGRAPH FROM ZAPRUDER FILM

PHOTOGRAPH FROM RE-ENACTMENT

PHOTOGRAPH THROUGH RIFLE SCOPE

DISTANCE TO STATION C .... 181.9 FT.

DISTANCE TO RIFLE IN WINDOW .... 218.0 FT.

ANGLE TO RIFLE IN WINDOW .... 18°03'

DISTANCE TO OVERPASS .... 307.1 FT.

ANGLE TO OVERPASS .... +0°44'

FRAME 255

Part of the exhibit from the Warren Commission Report. In the top left-hand corner, a frame from the Zapruder film shows Kennedy clutching his chest as a bullet strikes. At top right is a photo taken from the reenactment of the assassination. Bottom left shows how the presidential limousine was lined up in a rifle's telescopic site.

Undoubtedly that information would have led to new avenues of investigation, such as whether Castro had attempted to retaliate by murdering Kennedy.

Lyndon Johnson pressured the Warren Commission to issue its report before the 1964 presidential election, and this deadline did not encourage thoroughness. Rushed for time, commission investigators failed to follow up on numerous witnesses who claimed the shots had come from the grassy knoll, not from the School Book Depository. The report glossed over both Jack Ruby's mob connections and trips he had made to Cuba and failed to fully explain his unstable, violent nature. And quite glaringly, the commissioners could not develop a coherent motive for Oswald's actions.

Then there was the matter of physical evidence. Based on the Zapruder film, the Warren Commission found that the assassination had taken place in approximately five seconds. The commission, guided by assistant counsel Arlen Specter, believed Oswald had fired three shots—that one had missed and that one had taken

"Forgive My Grief"

Texas newspaperman Penn Jones, editor of the weekly *Midlothian Mirror*, charged that "every branch of the government had assisted in covering up and obfuscating the evidence left after that terrible weekend in Dallas."

His three *Forgive My Grief* books on the assassination focused on the supposedly large number of unnatural or suspicious deaths of assassination witnesses. By 1967 Jones had compiled a list of eighteen such unnatural deaths. Jones's charges were given added credence when in February of that year the prestigious *London Sunday Times* calculated that the odds of these deaths happening in the time frame Jones cited were 100,000 trillion to one. By 1983 Jones was contending there were "over 100 murders, suicides, and mysterious deaths, the strange fate of those who saw Kennedy shot."

Assassination figures and witnesses who met mysterious deaths included FBI director J. Edgar Hoover; a Ruby employee who committed suicide; the husband of another Ruby employee and a Dallas reporter who were murdered; a cleaning lady who saw a police car outside Oswald's rooming house just after the assassination; and prominent New York newspaper columnist Dorothy Kilgallen who had interviewed Jack Ruby. Jones wrote of Kilgallen: "Shortly before her death, Miss Kilgallen told a friend in New York that she was going to New Orleans in 5 days and break the case wide open."

Author Gerald Posner later analyzed the mysterious deaths issue. He noted that the *London Sunday Times* had admitted that the probability was nowhere near as astronomical as its published calculation and that it had committed "a careless journalistic mistake."

In fact, many of the hundred-plus mysterious deaths that Penn Jones had compiled weren't mysterious at all. The majority did not die for a full decade after the assassination. And many on the list were barely connected to the assassination.

off the top of the president's skull. That meant that the remaining shot had to have entered the president's back, exited his neck, and inflicted Governor Connally's five wounds (entrance and exit wounds to his back, chest, and left wrist and a flesh wound to his left thigh).

The Warren Report called this scenario the single-bullet theory. Even some of the seven-member commission were skeptical. Critics were soon saying it was ridiculous that a single bullet could have caused seven separate wounds and renamed it the magic-bullet theory.

Thirty years of controversy were about to begin.

The Doubts Begin

Almost from the very beginning, a growing band of assassination researchers picked through the commission's thousands of pages of exhibits, conducted their own interviews, and reached their own conclusions.

Mark Lane, a New York attorney and former member of the New York State Assembly, was among the first of many assassination researchers. A chance meeting with a New York City judge helped pique his interest in the Kennedy assassination. As they walked down a New York court house steps in the late afternoon of November 22, 1963, the jurist asked Lane if he thought Oswald killed the president. Then he answered his own question, referring to Parkland Hospital doctors' initial observations on Kennedy's wounds, saying, "He couldn't very well shoot him in the back and cause an entrance wound in his throat."

That chance remark inspired Lane to write and publish a defense brief that argued Oswald's innocence. Then he contacted the Warren Commission and volunteered to defend Oswald's interests before it. His offer was refused, but he continued digging into the case. In 1966 he published *Rush to Judgement*, which galvanized widespread public doubts about the Warren Report and stated that commission members had missed the importance of numerous key pieces of evidence. They were, argued Lane, "blinded by the fear of what they might see"—afraid that they might discover someone else besides Oswald had been involved in the assassination.

Rush to Judgement remained on the *New York Times* best-seller list for six months. In his review of the book, Pulitzer Prize–winning

Warren Commission critic Mark Lane points to a photo showing the route followed by President Kennedy. Lane contends that a second gunman fired shots from the bushes.

author Norman Mailer wrote: "If one-tenth of [the facts in *Rush to Judgement*] should prove to be significant, then the work of the Warren Commission will be judged to be a scandal worse than the Teapot Dome." (Teapot Dome was a notorious government scandal of President Warren Harding's administration in the early 1920s.)

Peabody Award–winning British journalist Alistair Cooke agreed, contending that Lane "had destroyed beyond a reasonable doubt the whole story of a single assassin."

Lane and his fellow researchers cast significant doubt on several key aspects of the Warren Report, including the reliability of eyewitness Howard Brennan, Oswald's marksmanship, the single-bullet theory, Oswald's palm print on the Mannlicher-Carcano found at the depository, how many shots had been fired and how fast, and whether shots had actually come from the depository or from the grassy knoll.

Maggie's Drawers

The quality of Oswald's marksmanship was one of Lane's disputes with the Warren Commission. He interviewed Nelson Delgado who had served with Oswald in the marines. Despite the fact that Oswald had once qualified as a sharpshooter, Delgado recalled that Oswald's marksmanship was "a big joke," noting that he had often missed the target completely causing a red flag, nicknamed Maggie's Drawers, to appear.

Delgado further stated that when FBI agents had interviewed him for the Warren Commission they worked hard to get him to

Oswald as a marine. Mark Lane disputed the Warren Commission's conclusion that Oswald had been a good enough shot to fire accurately enough to hit the president from his place at the School Book Depository.

48

back down from his opinion. "They attacked my competence to judge his character and shooting ability," he said.

Sherman Cooley, who trained in marine boot camp with Oswald, agreed with Delgado. "I saw that man [Oswald] shoot," Cooley told later researcher Henry Hurt in *Reasonable Doubt.* "There's no way he could have learned to shoot well enough to do what they accused him of doing in Dallas."

Howard Brennan

There were also questions regarding the Warren Commission's star eyewitness, Howard Brennan, who claimed to have seen Oswald at the School Book Depository's sixth-floor window. Brennan alleged that the man he saw was "standing up and resting against the left window sill." This was clearly impossible, as that floor's window ledges were far too low to allow a standing gunman to rest his rifle on the sills. Later Brennan saw Oswald in a police lineup and failed to make a positive identification. "He looks like the man, but I can't be sure." It was only after Oswald's death that he was willing to go on record definitely identifying Oswald. Brennan claimed he had been reluctant to finger Oswald because "if it got to be a known fact that I was an eyewitness, my family or I, either one, might not be safe."

The Latent Palm Print

Suspicions also pointed to the reliability of physical evidence in the case, and some skeptics wondered whether it was forged. On Saturday, November 23, the FBI announced that latent fingerprints found on Oswald's Mannlicher-Carcano rifle were "of no value." However, on November 29 the FBI received an Oswald palm print that Dallas police had lifted from the rifle's barrel on November 22.

David S. Lifton reported in *Best Evidence* that on November 24 FBI agents had fingerprinted Oswald while his body lay in a Dallas funeral parlor and hinted they used those prints to frame Oswald. "A postmortem palmprint," Lifton theorized, "could have been placed on the rifle at the Dallas morgue after 3:40 P.M., or later in Fort Worth."

Such a theory, however, lost much of its relevance in 1993 when the PBS *Frontline* program used new methods of scientific investigation to test the fingerprints the FBI called "of no value." They

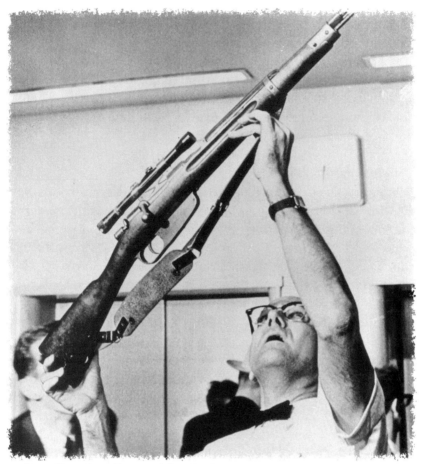

Police officers handle Oswald's rifle shortly after the assassination. Critics charged that the police had placed Oswald's prints on the gun after Oswald was dead.

found eighteen direct matching points between them and Lee Harvey Oswald's prints, enough for a positive identification linking Oswald directly to the rifle found in the School Book Depository.

The Grassy Knoll

The sounds of an assassin's rifle fire had reverberated throughout Dealey Plaza, making it difficult for even those present to determine exactly where they originated. Some witnesses thought they had come from the School Book Depository, some from the grassy knoll, others from the triple underpass. Others not only heard shots coming from the grassy knoll but also saw suspicious activities in its vicinity. The Warren Commission discounted their accounts. "No credible evidence," it concluded, "suggests that the shots were fired from the railroad bridge over the Triple Underpass, the nearby railroad yards or any other place than the Texas School Book Depository." The commission failed to call most of these dissenting witnesses to Washington for formal testimony. Mark Lane collected their stories and used them to cast serious doubt on the idea that Lee Harvey Oswald had indeed been the "lone assassin."

One of Lane's key witnesses was Jean Hill, a schoolteacher who was facing the grassy knoll as the shots rang out. In the Zapruder film she is the lady in red who can be seen clearly between the time Kennedy is shot for the first time and when he suffers his fatal head wound.

"I frankly thought they [the shots] were coming from the knoll . . .," Mrs. Hill recalled. "I thought it was just people shooting from the knoll—I did think there was more than one person shooting." She also testified she had seen a man in "a brown overcoat and hat" running from the knoll toward the railroad tracks to its rear.

Another important witness was Lee E. Bowers Jr., a railroad towerman who that day had a clear view of Dealey Plaza. Bowers reported that on the morning of November 22 he saw several cars driving suspiciously around the parking lot behind the grassy knoll. Immediately before the assassination Bowers observed two men behind the knoll's picket fence "within 10 or 15 feet of each other."

Bowers continued:

> At the time of the shooting, in the vicinity of where the two men I have described were, there was a flash of light, or as far as I am concerned, something I could not identify, but . . . which caught my eye in this immediate area of the embankment. Now what this was, I . . . could not identify it, other than some unusual occurrence—a flash of light or smoke or something which caused me to feel like something out of the ordinary happened.

J. C. Price was on the roof of the nearby Terminal Annex Building when Kennedy was shot. He told Lane he had seen a man running from the knoll and that this individual "was carrying something in his right hand [that] could have been a gun."

Sam M. Holland, who was atop the triple underpass when the shots rang out, also thought he saw "a puff of smoke come out

Ruby and the Police

One of the most puzzling aspects of the assassination was Jack Ruby's murder of Lee Harvey Oswald on national television in the presence of seventy to seventy-five members of the Dallas Police Department.

Not surprisingly, many observers suspected that Ruby might have secured the cooperation of some officers in killing Oswald. After all, not only was Oswald an accused presidential assassin, he was also a suspect in the murder of Officer Tippit.

The Dallas police denied any complicity in Ruby's actions, and Police Chief Jesse Curry denied persistent rumors that Ruby had long-standing ties to large numbers of local police. Curry "guessed" that "perhaps 25" and "less than 50 people [officers] knew him [Ruby]."

The Warren Report parroted this assertion, but Curry was clearly wrong. Lane produced numerous witnesses who contradicted him, including longtime Ruby associate William O'Donnell who estimated that Ruby was "on speaking terms with about 700 of the 1200 men on the police force" and that police officers were regularly provided with a "free round of drinks" when they visited the Carousel Club—in violation of local law. A rival nightclub owner told Lane that "it was common knowledge that Ruby spent time every day at the Dallas Police Department."

Were the police merely covering up their widespread (and often illegal) cozy relationship with a sleazy club owner? Or was something far more serious at stake?

Mark Lane wrote in *Rush to Judgement,* "No interpretation of November 24 can exclude the certainty that Ruby murdered Oswald through the complicity of members of the police."

about 6 or 8 feet above the ground right out from under those trees." He believed four and not three shots were fired and immediately headed for the fence to investigate further.

The Magic Bullet

Lane and the others who followed in his footsteps challenged the idea that a single bullet inflicted Kennedy's back and neck wounds and all of Connally's wounds. They questioned whether it was possible for a bullet traveling in a straight line to hit both Kennedy and Connally in the manner the Warren Commission claimed—or had this magic bullet zigzagged in midair? Supporting their contentions was John Connally's own conviction that he and Kennedy had been hit by separate shots. Connally's wife believed the same thing. If that were the case then *four* and not three shots had been fired. The Zapruder film had established a time frame for the assassination that would not allow for Oswald (or anyone else) to fire more than three shots from a Mannlicher-Carcano rifle. If more than three shots were fired, there were two assassins. Again, two assassins meant a conspiracy.

Lane also pointed to FBI tests of Oswald's Mannlicher-Carcano's capabilities. The FBI had three marksmen test fire it and concluded that Oswald could not have easily fired three shots at Kennedy. Lane wrote in *Rush to Judgement*:

> Only one expert [marksman] was able to get off three shots
> in the required period of time [4.8 to 5.6 seconds]. He fired
> three shots in 4.6 and 5.15 seconds. The other master rifle-

A man reenacts Oswald's part during a restaging of the Kennedy assassination. Many doubted the Warren Commission's finding that a single bullet had wounded both Connally and Kennedy.

men required 6.45, 6.75, 7.0 and 8.25 seconds, respectively. Not one of the 18 shots, regardless of the comparatively leisurely pace at which they were fired, struck the head or neck of the target.

Another issue calling the single-bullet theory into question was the weight of the so-called stretcher bullet (also known as Commission Exhibit 399 or CE 399). The Warren Commission had concluded that the stretcher bullet was the single bullet that had passed through both Kennedy and Connally. That bullet, found in a Parkland Memorial Hospital corridor, weighed 158.6 grains. If some fragments (some said as many as 3 grains) of it had been left behind in Kennedy's and Connally's bodies, then all the fragments added together weighed more than a normal cartridge should have. This discrepancy, contended the critics, was further proof that four shots had been fired.

Critics also pointed out that CE 399 was a pristine, or relatively undamaged, bullet. Mark Lane termed it "almost undeformed and unflattened." How could a bullet in such good shape have left fragments in Kennedy's and Connally's bodies? How could it have inflicted so much damage and not been significantly deformed?

4 Did a Group of Thrill Seekers Kill Kennedy?

In the first ten days after the Warren Commission Report was issued, over one million copies of it were sold, and its immediate result was an acceptance of the finding that a lone assassin had killed the president. But soon the questions were sprouting up again, particularly in New Orleans, where District Attorney Jim Garrison aggressively—and some would say irresponsibly—pursued the case.

New Orleans district attorney Jim Garrison investigated and formulated his own controversial opinions about the Kennedy assassination.

Ice Skating in Texas

On November 24, two days after the assassination, New Orleans private detective Jack Martin phoned the district attorney's office to report that he had a lead on the accused killer. Martin believed that after the assassination, one of his friends, David W. Ferrie, had flown a plane to retrieve Oswald, an accomplice in Kennedy's death, in Dallas. He believed Ferrie and Oswald were connected when he realized that Ferrie had driven from New Orleans to Texas on the day of the assassination.

On a radio news broadcast Martin learned of Oswald's involvement in the New Orleans Civil Air Patrol (CAP); he knew that Ferrie had also belonged to the CAP in the 1950s. Was Ferrie, an accomplished pilot, heading for Dallas to fly a getaway plane for

The bizarre-looking David Ferrie, who Garrison believed was part of a plot to help Oswald escape. Garrison contended that Ferrie was to fly a getaway plane with Oswald aboard.

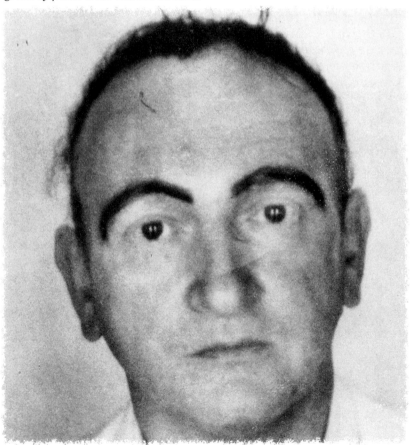

The Bishop of New Orleans

David Ferrie was clearly the most bizarre character ever to be linked to the Kennedy assassination.

Ferrie had once studied for the Roman Catholic priesthood. He and Jack Martin were the only two members of a tiny sect they created and called the American Orthodox Old Catholic Church of North America, an offshoot of Catholicism. Ferrie considered himself a bishop of that church.

He was a man of many interests and claimed to have a doctorate in psychology and to be a master hypnotist. His New Orleans apartment housed three thousand books and hundreds of mice. The mice were there for experiments he was conducting to find a cure for cancer. Once a pilot for Eastern Airlines, Ferrie allegedly made several landings in Cuba before the Bay of Pigs operation and was considered to be heavily involved in anti-Castro guerrilla operations.

Ferrie suffered from a disease that left him totally hairless. Jim Garrison remembered his first meeting with the enigmatic Ferrie. "The face grinning ferociously at me was a ghoulish Halloween mask," he wrote. "The eyebrows were greasepaint, one noticeably higher than the other. A scruffy, reddish homemade wig hung askew on his head as he fixed me with his eyes."

Oswald? District Attorney Jim Garrison's office immediately swung into action. Under questioning, Ferrie admitted he had indeed traveled to Texas on November 22, but not to Dallas. He had instead driven to Houston and then to Galveston with two teenaged friends—to go ice skating. Garrison was suspicious of Ferrie's story. Ferrie had driven all the way to Texas, but he had not gone skating. Instead, he made and received several calls from pay phones. What, wondered Garrison, was the trip really about?

"A Swinging Cat"

Soon other New Orleans connections were popping up. Further piquing Garrison's interest were comments made privately to him by U.S. senator Russell Long, himself the son of an assassinated politician. "There's no way in the world that one man could have shot Jack Kennedy that way," Long told Garrison.

Attorney Dean Andrews claimed that Oswald was part of a conspiracy to kill Kennedy. But Andrews proved an unreliable witness, finally disclaiming his testimony, saying he had been high on drugs at the time.

Meanwhile, New Orleans attorney Dean Andrews had informed the Warren Commission that in 1963 Oswald had visited his office "a maximum of five times," to discuss a variety of legal matters, including his and his wife's citizenship and his dishonorable discharge. Andrews stated that Oswald was always in the presence of a "Mexicano" and occasionally was accompanied by "some gay kids." Andrews also claimed that his office was broken into and that papers relating to Oswald's visits were stolen.

Andrews, a colorful figure, also told the commission that on the day following the assassination he received a call from a mysterious client requesting him to fly to Dallas and serve as Lee Harvey Oswald's defense attorney.

The caller identified himself as Clay Bertrand.

Yet Andrews could not identify Bertrand, which he said was an alias. Andrews further claimed he had seen Bertrand only once and gave two wildly different descriptions of him. He told the Warren Commission that Bertrand was five feet eight with sandy hair; he told the FBI that Bertrand was six feet one with brown hair. Of one thing Andrews was sure, "Bertrand [was] bisexual. What they call a swinging cat."

Andrews would later deny everything, telling Warren Commission investigators he was "smoking dope . . . full of dope" when he reported on Bertrand, who he now said was totally fictitious. But Jim Garrison wasn't sure about that. He was starting to think that a number of things were coming together. Ferrie and Oswald had been in the Civilian Air Patrol. Oswald had given his office address as 544 Camp Street, which actually housed private detective Guy Banister's office and a Cuban exile group, the Cuban Revolutionary Council. Ferrie and Banister had known each other and were both rabid anticommunists. And Ferrie and the mysterious Clay Bertrand were both homosexuals. Garrison put these coincidences together and began to create a theory of conspiracy to kill Kennedy.

But Garrison still had no proof. He had to find Bertrand.

"A Coup Can Be Unstoppable"

In his 1988 book, *On the Trail of the Assassins*, Jim Garrison blamed Kennedy's assassination on segments of JFK's Praetorian guard, a reference to those troops entrusted with guarding Roman emperors:

> In the United States the modern counterparts to the Praetorian Guard are the secret police of the intelligence community, beginning with the smallish, close-at-hand Secret Service and extending on through the F.B.I., the intelligence divisions of various federal departments, the Defense Intelligence Agency, and the Central Intelligence Agency. Without key elements of this modern-day Praetorian Guard, a coup d'etat in the United States would be impossible. With them, however, a coup can be unstoppable.

Representative of Humanity

As the trial of Clay Shaw drew to a close, District Attorney Jim Garrison may have realized how weak his case against the New Orleans businessman was. In his twenty-five minute summation to the jury, he mentioned Shaw's name just once. But he did make a powerful appeal to the emotions regarding the slain ex-president. He concluded:

> The murder of John F. Kennedy was probably the most terrible moment in the history of our country. Yet, circumstances have placed you in the position where not only have you seen the hidden evidence but you are actually going to have the same opportunity to bring justice into the picture for the first time.
>
> Now, you are sitting in judgment of Clay Shaw. Yet you, as men, represent more than jurors in an ordinary case because of the victim in this case. You represent, in a sense, the hope of humanity, which may yet triumph over excessive governmental power—if you will cause it to be so, in the course of doing your duty in this case.
>
> I suggest that you ask not what your country can do for you but what you can do for your country.
>
> What can you do for your country? You can cause justice to happen for the first time in this matter. You can help make our country better by showing that this is still a government of the people. And if you do that, as long as you live, nothing will ever be more important.

"A Perfect Crime"

By late 1966 Garrison had suspicions that Bertrand was actually white-haired, six-feet four-inch Clay Shaw, a prominent New Orleans businessman, the managing director of the New Orleans International Trade Mart, an organization designed to increase that city's foreign trade, particularly with Latin America. Shaw, like

Bertrand, was gay, and Garrison would soon come to believe that a homosexual conspiracy was behind the JFK killing.

Garrison kept after Ferrie, whom he would call "one of history's most important individuals," keeping him under surveillance and hoping he would break. Then on Wednesday, February 22, 1967, Ferrie's lifeless body was found in his New Orleans apartment. The cause of death was ruled "natural causes," a berry aneurism, a bursting of a blood vessel in his head. But two suspicious type-written notes telling of Ferrie's weariness with life were found on the premises. "To leave this life is, for me, a sweet prospect," he had written in one. "I find nothing in it that is desirable and on the other hand, everything that is loathsome." Many thought Ferrie had committed suicide, although some believed the notes might have been planted by Garrison's office.

Garrison discovered one witness, David Lewis, who was willing to testify that he had seen Shaw, Oswald, Ferrie, and Banister at an anti-Castro meeting in 1962. Lewis's account, however, couldn't be true: Oswald wasn't in New Orleans in 1962. He was either in the Soviet Union or, later in the year, in Texas. Garrison needed a new witness to keep his investigation alive.

Clay Shaw arrives at criminal court after being accused by Jim Garrison of taking part in a conspiracy to kill Kennedy.

He got one just two days after Ferrie's death when a twenty-five-year-old Baton Rouge insurance agent named Perry Raymond Russo told television reporters that he had known Ferrie and that Ferrie had vehemently disliked Kennedy. Under later questioning Russo told Garrison's investigators that he participated in a discussion with Ferrie and a Clem Bertrand, whom he identified as Shaw, and that the assassination of John Kennedy had indeed been discussed.

Garrison finally had his case—and added a nonpolitical factor to the mix. He informed a *Saturday Evening Post* reporter that: "It was a homosexual thrill-killing, plus the excitement of getting away with a perfect crime. John Kennedy was everything that Dave Ferrie was not—a successful, handsome, popular, wealthy, virile man."

On March 1, 1967, Clay Shaw was arrested for conspiring to murder John F. Kennedy.

Crossfire

On March 14, 1967, a preliminary hearing was held to determine if there was enough evidence to bring Shaw to trial. Perry Russo, the key witness, shocked the nation with his testimony of an assassination conspiracy. Russo told the court that "somewhere around the middle of 1963" he had been at a party at David Ferrie's apartment. Among those present was Clem Bertrand, a "white hair[ed]" man matching Clay Shaw's description. Also in attendance was Ferrie's roommate, a Leon Oswald, although Russo was not sure that this was Lee Harvey Oswald. After the other guests left, the quartet discussed killing Castro, and then the conversation turned to talk of assassinating Kennedy. None of those present liked Kennedy (Perry later admitted that he "hated" him), and the group theorized that if Kennedy were killed, the act could be blamed on Castro and used as an excuse to invade Cuba. Ferrie argued that with the help of "diversionary tactics" JFK could be caught in a "triangulation of crossfire." Ferrie and Bertrand even discussed establishing highly visible alibis for the date and time of the Kennedy assassination.

Garrison's second major witness was a black man, Vernon Bundy, who testified that in July 1963 he had seen Shaw and Oswald together at the Lake Pontchartrain seawall, a retaining wall at Louisiana's largest lake. Shaw gave Oswald what looked like "a roll

Perry Raymond Russo (pictured) claimed that he heard Shaw plotting with Oswald and Ferrie to murder Kennedy.

of money." At the preliminary hearing Bundy dramatically pointed a finger to identify Clay Shaw as the man he saw with Oswald.

On March 22, 1967, a grand jury indicted Clay Shaw for conspiring with Oswald, Ferrie, "and others" to murder JFK.

The Jury Decides

Garrison now shifted his investigation from New Orleans to Dallas, using an army of private researchers to expand his assassination inquiry, building on the idea of triangulated fire in Dealey Plaza

Vernon Bundy testified that he had seen Oswald and Clay Shaw together and that Shaw had given Oswald a roll of money.

and theories that Kennedy was a victim of America's military in-dustrial complex because of his disagreements with the CIA and the possibility that he might withdraw U.S. armed forces from South Vietnam.

Russo and Bundy repeated their charges at Shaw's trial, and a New York accountant named Charles Spiesel testified that in the summer of 1963 he had been at a New Orleans party with both Shaw and Ferrie, who openly discussed their plans to murder JFK.

Garrison also produced six witnesses who said they had seen Oswald, Ferrie, and Shaw together at a Congress of Racial Equality (CORE) black-voter registration drive in Clinton, Louisiana, 130 miles from New Orleans.

The prosecution additionally presented two witnesses to sup-port its contention that Clay Shaw had used the alias Bertrand. A mailman said he had delivered mail bearing the name of Clem

Bertrand to Shaw. A hostess at the New Orleans airport produced a guest registry bearing the signature Clay Bertrand, which she claimed Shaw had signed.

The district attorney further produced a New Orleans police officer named Aloysius J. Habinghorst, who was willing to swear that when he booked Shaw for the Kennedy assassination, the suspect admitted to using the alias Clay Bertrand. Habinghorst dutifully filled that information in his paperwork.

That was the New Orleans phase of Garrison's argument. But in order to prove a conspiracy was at work he also attempted to disprove the Warren Commission's contention that Lee Harvey Oswald had acted alone. He subpoenaed the Zapruder film, which had been purchased by the Time-Life Company and was then generally unavailable for public showing. Garrison screened it ten times for jury members, showing them how Kennedy's head had jerked backwards, thus indicating that the fatal shot had come not from the Texas School Book Depository to the president's rear, but

Prosecution by Hypnosis

Americans were stunned when they learned how Jim Garrison had obtained Perry Russo's revelations of a conspiracy to kill President Kennedy.

After Russo had first been interviewed by Assistant District Attorney Andrew Sciambra on February 25, 1967, Sciambra wrote a thirty-five-hundred-word memo to Garrison detailing Russo's allegations. It contained no hint whatsoever that Ferrie, Clem Bertrand, and Lee Oswald had ever discussed assassinating Kennedy. It was only two days later, however, after being injected with sodium pentothal, or truth serum, and being carefully coached and subjected to hypnotism by Dr. Esmond Fatter who had no experience in using hypnosis in a criminal prosecution, that Russo supplied Sciambra with information about a conspiracy. It was, in fact, Dr. Fatter who first suggested to Russo that the people at the gathering were "talking about assassinating somebody."

Dr. Fatter himself later admitted that he "certainly would hate to see anyone taken to trial on what Russo had said in a trance."

rather from the *front* of the presidential motorcade. If there were two assassins, there clearly had to be a conspiracy to murder the president.

Garrison's prosecution team presented eyewitnesses who swore they had seen Kennedy's head snap back, thus indicating he had been hit from the front. They also presented "earwitnesses" who heard gunfire coming from the grassy knoll. Garrison hacked away at the single-bullet theory, arguing that one bullet could not have produced all of Kennedy's and Connally's wounds.

Also testifying was Dallas County deputy sheriff Roger D. Craig who claimed he saw Oswald leave the School Book Depository and

"This Gross Mistake"

Many observers continue to question whether Lee Harvey Oswald could have hit a target below and moving away from him.

What if he couldn't hit such a target? What if he actually had missed? What if he wasn't actually aiming at Kennedy?

Oswald had been honorably discharged from the U.S. Marines in September 1959, but after he violated its terms and defected to the Soviet Union his discharge was changed to a dishonorable one. This infuriated him. On January 30, 1962, Oswald wrote to the American secretary of the navy (the Department of the Navy has jurisdiction over the marines) from the USSR, warning that he would "employ all means to right this gross mistake or injustice to a bona-fide U.S. citizen and ex-serviceman."

That secretary of the navy was John Connally.

A year after the assassination, Marina Oswald commented that she thought her husband "was shooting at Connally rather than President Kennedy."

Yet, like so much concerning the events in Dallas, problems exist with that theory as well. Oswald spoke well of Connally and once even told Marina that he would vote for the conservative Democrat for governor of Texas. If Oswald was aiming at Connally, he could not have picked a worse time to do it, as once the motorcade had passed the School Book Depository Kennedy was almost totally blocking Oswald's view of Connally.

Clay Shaw holds a New Orleans newspaper that proclaims his innocence. The jury found Garrison's case to be based on rumor and speculation.

get into a light colored Nash Rambler station wagon driven by an Hispanic-looking man. Clearly, contended Garrison, a conspiracy had been at work, and Clay Shaw had been at the heart of it.

On March 1, 1969, two years to the day after Shaw's original arrest, Jim Garrison rested his case against him. Just forty-five minutes later the jury returned its verdict: Shaw was innocent of any conspiracy to murder John F. Kennedy.

"Genuine Lunatic Testimony"

What went wrong with Jim Garrison's case? The answer was just about everything.

Perry Russo, while still claiming that Ferrie, Oswald, and Shaw had been together at Ferrie's party, suddenly wavered on whether they were serious about killing Kennedy. Two witnesses that Russo said were at the party refused to verify his testimony. A New Orleans police lieutenant testified that Russo admitted to him that the white-haired man at the party was probably not Shaw. Russo later confided to a reporter that he feared that if he had withdrawn any more of his testimony Garrison would indict him for perjury.

Vernon Bundy turned out to be an inmate of the New Orleans Parish prison, and two fellow prisoners testified he had boasted of perjuring himself for Garrison, "because that's the only way" he could get out of jail. On the stand Bundy, a heroin addict, admitted that he was injecting the drug into his veins when he "saw" Shaw at Lake Pontchartrain in July 1963.

Charles Spiesel became completely unhinged during his testimony, contending that he had been "hypnotized or tortured" fifty or sixty times by New York City police and members of his accounting firm. He was so paranoid and suspicious of plots against him that he once fingerprinted his own daughter to ensure it was actually her and not an impostor. Even Garrison had to admit Spiesel's performance was "an unforgettable example of genuine lunatic testimony."

Dean Andrews, who had triggered Garrison's interest in Clay Bertrand, admitted Shaw was not "Bertrand," and furthermore that the whole Bertrand story was a "figment of [his] imagination."

The trial judge ruled that Aloysius Habinghorst had violated Shaw's rights by not informing him of those rights when booking him. He further stated he thought Habinghorst was lying and refused to allow him to testify.

The press and the public were outraged by Garrison's circuslike prosecution of Shaw. The *New Orleans States-Item* called the district attorney a "man without principle" who should resign from office. The *New York Times* labeled the episode "one of the most disgraceful chapters in the history of American jurisprudence." NBC television, led by former Robert Kennedy aide Walter Sheridan, investigated Garrison's methods and concluded his case was "an enormous fraud," based on "bribery and intimidation of witnesses."

"In the final analysis," noted Henry Hurt in *Reasonable Doubt,* "Jim Garrison never proved a single point in court against Clay Shaw."

Yet other researchers continued their work, and the American public continued to doubt the official explanation of the assassination.

The Intelligence Theories

Once investigators such as Jim Garrison and Mark Lane raised doubts about the thoroughness and conclusions of the Warren Commission Report, other researchers and theorists began filling in the blanks on why the assassination had really taken place and who had been involved. Evidence of previously concealed government contacts with Oswald became public, and the questions mounted. Much speculation revolved around whether Oswald was connected to such agencies as the CIA, FBI, KGB, or U.S. military intelligence.

Was Oswald a Spy?

Assassination researchers also pointed out the mysterious role the CIA and military intelligence played in the Lee Harvey Oswald story. Reports of these spy agencies popped up again and again.

Colonel L. Fletcher Prouty, a former air force liaison officer to the CIA, reported that the 112th Military Intelligence Group (MIG), a spy agency similar to the CIA based at San Antonio's Fort Houston, wanted to augment the president's security in Dallas, but was instead ordered to stand down on November 22, 1963.

Immediately after the assassination, Lieutenant Colonel Robert E. Jones of the 112th MIG learned from his agents in Dallas that A. J. Hidell had been arrested for Kennedy's murder. He checked his unit's files and found that Hidell was an alias for Oswald.

The House Select Committee on Assassinations concluded that Jones's testimony "suggested the existence of a military intelligence file on Oswald and raised the possibility that he had intelligence associations [that is, possibly with military intelligence or the CIA]."

Despite requests for such information, no such files were ever provided to the Warren Commission. When the House Committee

Colonel L. Fletcher Prouty contended that the Military Intelligence Group had been told to stand down when it wanted to help with the president's security in Dallas.

on Assassinations learned about these files in 1975, they were told they had been "destroyed routinely in accordance with normal files management procedures" in 1973.

Regarding the loss of this highly significant material the committee wrote:

> The committee found this "routine" destruction of the Oswald file extremely troublesome, especially when viewed in light of the Department of Defense's failure to make the file available to the Warren Commission. Despite the credibility of Jones' testimony, without access to this file, the question of Oswald's possible affiliation with military intelligence could not be fully resolved.

The U-2 Incident

To all intents and purposes Lee Harvey Oswald was a classic loser—a high school dropout in low-paying menial jobs, who despite his intellectual pretensions, could barely spell. He had never had a driver's license nor owned a car.

Yet, many wondered whether there was far more to Oswald than appeared on the surface. After all, even before the Kennedy assassination his life had been extremely unusual. He not only defected to the Soviet Union. He had defected back. His wife was the niece of an MVD officer. There was no question that he had contacts with the Cuban embassy in Mexico City, pro-Castro Americans, and anti-Castro Cuban exiles. Could Oswald have been some sort of deeply placed intelligence operative?

Some thought he had been recruited as an FBI agent while in the marines. But the question was: by whom? Some pointed to his knowledge of the Russian language and theorized that the U.S. government had taught him that language to prepare him to serve as one of its operatives. Nelson Delgado, the marine who recalled Oswald's poor marksmanship, remembered that Oswald spoke of

Some conspiracy theorists believed that Oswald may have been recruited as an FBI agent while he was a marine.

The Accidental Assassination

Baltimore gunsmith Howard Donahue conceived one of the most unusual assassination theories yet. Unlike the others, however, it involved no conspiracies with the Mafia, the CIA, or the FBI, and found no contact between Oswald and Ruby.

It did involve one member of the Secret Service acting alone.

Originally, Donahue had started his investigation of the Kennedy assassination believing in the accuracy of the Warren Report. But he soon faced a problem. Oswald's Mannlicher-Carcano rifle fired a 6.5-millimeter bullet, yet the Warren Report stated that the entrance wound in Kennedy's skull was only 6 millimeters in diameter.

How could a bullet create a smaller hole than the bullet itself?

Donahue finally came up with an answer. In his view Secret Service agent George Hickey riding in the Secret Service follow-up car—just twenty-four feet away from the president—reacted to Oswald's first shot. He jumped up off the seat of the moving vehicle and fell backwards. As he did his AR-15 rifle went off, hitting Kennedy in the head and ultimately killing him. An AR-15 round of ammunition has a diameter of 5.56 millimeters, thus fitting nicely with Donahue's conjecture.

Yet, there were problems with Donahue's theory. Actually, the entrance wound being slightly smaller than the bullet was explained by the so-called elastic recoil of the skull. Even Donahue had to admit in his book *Mortal Error: The Shot That Killed JFK* that "the entrance hole diameter proof was less than conclusive." And there was not a single eyewitness to corroborate that Hickey had actually fired a shot that day. Rifles, after all, are not silent. They make noise, a lot of it.

Said Kennedy aide Dave Powers, who was in the car right next to Hickey, "The point is, . . . someone a foot away from me to two feet away from me couldn't fire the gun without me hearing it."

going to Cuba and fighting for the Castro revolution. Furthermore, Delgado claimed that Oswald received mail from the Cuban consulate and indicated that he had written to them also.

In the marines, Oswald was given the sensitive post of radar controller stationed at the Atsugi Air Force Base in Japan where the top secret American spy planes were stationed. Oswald's work at Atsugi took on increased significance on May 1, 1960, when a U-2 was shot down on a secret mission over the Soviet Union. The incident had grave international repercussions and caused the embarrassing cancellation of a planned Paris summit meeting between Soviet premier Khrushchev and President Dwight Eisenhower. The U-2 mission originated in Atsugi.

The pilot was taken prisoner. His Soviet interrogators seemed knowledgeable about Atsugi. Had they learned about it from Oswald, who had moved to the Soviet Union in 1959? When Oswald defected he warned American embassy officials that he would give the Soviets radar secrets of "special interest."

The entire issue of Oswald's defection and return raised additional questions.

Programmed by the CIA? A Soviet Spy?

Was Oswald's defection genuine or was it planned by military intelligence or the CIA? Why had none of his marine superiors been concerned over his studying Russian or his vocal procommunist sympathies? Was his presence at Atsugi a mere coincidence? And why did the United States allow him to return after he had defected and tried to renounce his citizenship? After returning to the United States, were his contacts with pro- and anti-Castro groups mere covers for CIA activities?

Officially Oswald had returned home because of disillusionment with the Soviet system: "The work is drab. The money I get has nowhere to be spent. No nightclubs or bowling alleys. No places of recreation except the trade union dances. I have had enough." Or did he return home because he had been recruited as a Soviet spy?

Had Soviet intelligence enlisted him as an agent and ordered him back? Those who believed in this theory pointed to Oswald's private apartment in Minsk, a luxurious rarity for ordinary Soviets. They were suspicious of Oswald's whirlwind courtship of his wife

Marina and pointed out that her uncle was an MVD official with ties to Soviet intelligence. They wondered why the Soviets, who kept millions of their citizens from leaving the USSR, allowed Lee and Marina Oswald to leave so easily.

The Spy Who Knew About Oswald

Less than two months after the Kennedy assassination Soviet KGB official Yuri Nosenko defected to the United States. On arriving he made a startling claim: while in the USSR he had worked on Lee Harvey Oswald's files.

Nosenko informed the CIA that the KGB had "absolutely no interest" in Oswald. Soviet doctors had determined that Oswald was "mentally unstable" and "should be avoided at all costs." Oswald was allowed to stay in the USSR only because of his suicide attempt. The Soviets feared that a suicide might create an international incident. The KGB avoided contact with Oswald (although it did monitor his activities) and was only too happy to see him leave and return to the United States.

The CIA didn't believe Nosenko. They feared he was a Soviet agent sent to mislead Americans about whether a high-ranking counterspy, or mole, was active in the CIA. American intelligence attempted to break Nosenko, to force him to admit he was still a Soviet agent. To make Nosenko talk they locked him in a Washington area attic for sixteen months under barbaric conditions. For four more months he was kept in solitary confinement inside a windowless ten-by-ten-foot concrete bunker. His story never changed. It was not until September 1968 that the CIA finally admitted that Nosenko was a genuine defector who was telling the truth.

Microdots

When Oswald returned to the United States he found employment at the Jaggars-Chiles-Stovall Company, a Dallas typesetting firm. Most of the work the company performed was for magazines, newspapers, and assorted advertisers, but it also held a contract from the Army Map Service to produce maps made from highly classified sources, such as the U-2. Many wondered how a figure like Oswald could receive a security clearance at such an operation. Fueling their concern was a cryptic notation discovered in his personal address book: "microdot." Was Oswald using microdots, extremely tiny photographic negatives, to record information found at Jaggars-Chiles-Stovall and pass it on to Soviet intelligence?

Others have pointed out that Oswald had no access to any classified material at Jaggars-Chiles-Stovall and wondered why, if he were engaged in espionage there, he jeopardized his intelligence mission with a job performance so "inefficient [and] . . . inept" that he was fired in April 1963.

Oswald and the Baron

One of Oswald's few friends in Dallas was a world-traveling oil geologist of Russian aristocratic stock named George de Mohrenschildt. Sorting out the truth about the mysterious de Mohrenschildt, who claimed to be a baron, was difficult. He has variously been connected to Nazi, Polish, British, and French intelligence services,

George de Mohrenschildt was a world-traveling, sophisticated aristocrat. Conspiracy theorists wondered why he was good friends with someone like Lee Harvey Oswald.

and it is known that he had reported to the CIA's contract division regarding trips he made to Mexico, Panama, and to communist Yugoslavia.

Many wondered why this sophisticated businessman (his address book contained the home phone number of fellow Texas oilman and future president George H. W. Bush) would bother to associate with a failure like Oswald. Some have argued that de Mohrenschildt was a CIA control agent, or handler, for Oswald, that is, his espionage superior.

By early 1977 de Mohrenschildt had revealed to author Edward Jay Epstein that the CIA had asked him to watch Oswald. The House Select Committee on Assassinations wanted to question de Mohrenschildt. By then, however, de Mohrenschildt's mental health had seriously deteriorated. Ironically, he had once been confined in Parkland Hospital's psychiatric unit.

On March 29, 1977, de Mohrenschildt committed suicide by blowing his head off with a 20-gauge shotgun. Some assassination researchers, however, hinted that de Mohrenschildt had actually been silenced by alleged conspirators.

The Castro Connection

It was not only those outside government who had doubts about the Warren Report. Commission member Senator Richard Russell, who later also chaired the Senate CIA Oversight Committee, said he "thought someone else worked with" Oswald. Lyndon Johnson had his own theory. LBJ was convinced Fidel Castro was involved in the assassination. In interviews with CBS newscaster Walter Cronkite and ABC newscaster Howard K. Smith, Johnson revealed that he was concerned that Castro, motivated by a sense of revenge over CIA plots to kill him, had instigated a counterplot to kill JFK.

Johnson, while president, however, was extremely nervous about such a theory becoming widespread, fearing it would increase international tensions and perhaps even lead to nuclear war against either Cuba or the Soviet Union. Adding to his suspicions were reports of a November 27, 1963, speech in which Castro said "the first time Oswald was in Cuba . . ." However, those reports were in error. Castro actually was speaking about Oswald's visit to the Cuban consulate in Mexico City.

Cuba, Vietnam, and the CIA

The Warren Commission never established a clear motive to explain Lee Harvey Oswald's murder of John Kennedy.

But many assassination researchers, including Jim Garrison, thought they had found one: dissatisfaction with Kennedy's policies regarding Cuba, Vietnam, and the CIA.

In 1961 the CIA-planned invasion of Cuba failed. Many within the CIA blamed John Kennedy for failing to provide needed air cover as anti-Castro guerrillas landed on the beach at Cuba's Bay of Pigs. For his part Kennedy was outraged by the CIA's handling of the botched affair and threatened to strip the agency of its "exorbitant power."

Many anticommunists were also angered by Kennedy's handling of the 1962 Cuban missile crisis, suspecting that JFK had made a deal with Soviet dictator Nikita Khrushchev. They believed the Soviet missiles were removed from Castro's island in exchange for a U.S. pledge to stop trying to overthrow Castro. Cuban exiles bitterly complained they had been betrayed.

In addition, Kennedy seemed to be wearying of U.S. involvement in Vietnam. In October 1963 Kennedy signed NSAM 263, giving orders to Secretary of Defense Robert McNamara to withdraw one thousand U.S. military advisers from that embattled country. Would Kennedy have prevented a war that the military-industrial complex wanted in order to strengthen their own interests?

In March 1964 Lyndon Johnson signed NSAM 288, which rescinded Kennedy's order to begin withdrawing U.S. forces from Vietnam.

In *On the Trail of the Assassins*, Jim Garrison wrote:

> While it was difficult for me to accept that an entire agency as enormous as the C.I.A. could have sanctioned and carried out a plan to assassinate the President, it did not seem unreasonable that rogue elements within the Agency or contract agents who might have been working with them on other projects might well have.

Oswald in Mexico

In September 1963 Lee Harvey Oswald traveled by Continental Trailways bus to Mexico City to arrange for his next defection, this time to Fidel Castro's Cuba. The CIA normally kept the Cuban embassy under surveillance and photographed persons entering and leaving it; the photos should have included Oswald. On October 10, 1963, the CIA issued a bulletin regarding Oswald to the FBI, the U.S. Department of State, and the navy. He was described as "approximately 35 years old, with an athletic build, about six feet tall, with a receding hairline . . ." This was clearly *not* Oswald. Later the CIA produced the photos of a man they thought was Oswald. It was not.

Some assassination researchers have concluded that there were two Oswalds, the genuine article and a U.S. intelligence manufactured one. The two-Oswald theory is supported by those who believe that Oswald was blamed for a crime he did not commit.

According to conspiracy buffs, the mysterious figures who framed Oswald may have been CIA or military intelligence agents or even right-wing oil millionaires. In their minds, the false Oswald may have been sent to Mexico City merely to create the appearance of pro-Castro sympathies on Oswald's part. "Oswald probably never went to Mexico City and visited the Cuban and Soviet embassies there . . .," allege authors Robert Groden and Harrison Edward Livingstone in *High Treason*. "This evidence was deliberately fabricated by the people who set Oswald up as the patsy in the assassination of President Kennedy."

Others have settled on a far simpler explanation: govern-

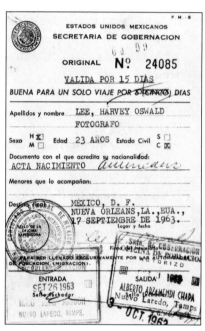

A visa authorizes Lee Harvey Oswald to visit Mexico. Oswald traveled to Mexico City in 1963 ostensibly to gain permission to travel to Cuba. Conspiracy theorists believe he may never have gone there.

mental incompetence. CIA cameras outside the embassy did not operate at all times; the agents simply guessed which person entering the Cuban embassy was Oswald and guessed wrong.

Later, Cuban embassy officials confirmed that the Oswald that they met with was the real Lee Harvey Oswald. But that left the question: Who was the man in the CIA photos? Oleg Maximovich Nechiporenko, a KGB colonel stationed at the Soviet embassy, identified the second Oswald as a mentally unstable former U.S. serviceman who would occasionally wander into his embassy.

Invasion of the Body Snatchers

One of the most sensational of all assassination theories was developed by David S. Lifton in his best-selling book *Best Evidence.*

Under Texas law John F. Kennedy's body should never have left the state before an autopsy was performed. Yet, because of the extraordinary nature of events, it was quickly put in a coffin and placed on *Air Force One.* When the body arrived in Washington, it was transported to Bethesda Naval Hospital in suburban Maryland where a team of doctors concluded that two bullets had struck the president. Both bullets entered his body from the rear. The first had struck him in the back and exited through his neck; the second savagely ripped open his skull and killed him.

However, as Parkland doctors tried to save Kennedy's life, they had identified his throat wound as an entrance wound. Many wondered why such a startling—and critical—difference of opinions existed.

Lifton set out to reconcile the two pieces of information. He concluded that Kennedy had been shot in the throat from the *front*—and that somewhere between Dallas and Washington JFK's body had been snatched away and that his wounds had been surgically altered to conform to official version of events that both shots had come from the rear. One shot coming from the front and one from the back would certainly indicate a conspiracy. On the other hand, if both shots had come from the front, Oswald could not have been the only assassin.

An important piece of evidence presented by Lifton involves the casket in which Kennedy's body was transported from Dallas to Washington. A variety of photographs taken in Dallas show the casket containing Kennedy's body to be an expensive, burnished-bronze casket. Yet Lifton produced witnesses in the Washington

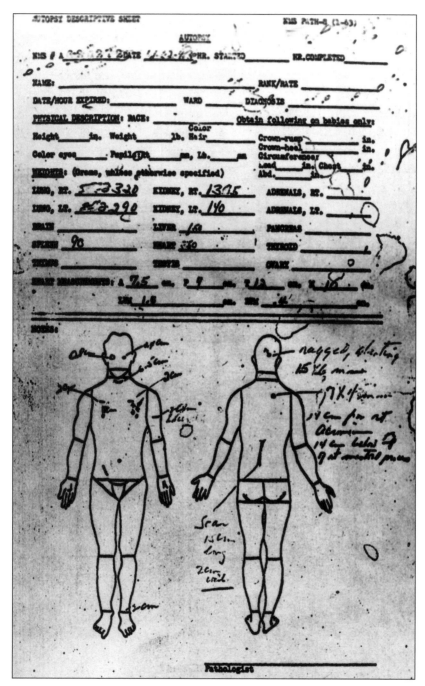

A diagram that appeared in the Warren Commission Report shows the entrance and exit wounds of the bullets that hit President Kennedy. Some theorize that the bullet that hit Kennedy's throat had to have entered through the front, proving that there were two assassins.

area who testified that the casket they saw was a cheap, military-style casket. He also found two hospital technicians who informed him that JFK's body had arrived at Bethesda in a simple body bag.

A grief-stricken Jackie Kennedy had accompanied her husband's coffin from Parkland Hospital to *Air Force One* and remained with it virtually the entire time until the plane touched down in Washington. When could the body have been removed from its original coffin?

Lifton contended that Kennedy's casket was left unattended from 2:18 P.M. until 2:32 P.M., just prior to Lyndon Johnson's taking the presidential oath of office at 2:38. Kennedy's body was then

"Malarkey"

David Lifton's theory of the president's body being removed from its coffin and having its wounds surgically altered has triggered harsh criticism. Robert Groden and Harrison Edward Livingstone in their *High Treason* point out that such surgery would have taken hours and could not have been done in the time frame Lifton constructs.

They also quote the president's aide and close friend Dave Powers:

> The coffin was never left unattended. Lifton's story is the biggest pack of malarkey I ever heard in my life. I never had my hands or eyes off of it during the period he says it was unattended, and when Jackie [Kennedy] got up to go to the stateroom where Lyndon Johnson was . . . we stayed right with the coffin and never let go of it. In fact several of us were with it through the whole trip, all the way to Bethesda Hospital.

Gerald Posner in *Case Closed* points out that over the years other Lifton theories have included spotting the following on the grassy knoll: "a man with a Kaiser Wilhelm helmet, another with an electronic headset, one with a periscope and another with a machine gun hidden in a hydraulic lift. He thought one of the men resembled General Douglas MacArthur."

The casket containing the body of John Kennedy is moved to a navy ambulance from the presidential plane. David Lifton contends that Kennedy's body was left unattended for fourteen minutes, during which time someone tampered with the body to disguise the evidence.

hastily placed in the body bag. "Disguised as luggage," Lifton wrote, "it might have been put in the baggage hold, or in the forward galley area" so as to allow for it to later be taken to a secret destination and surgically altered.

Lifton believes that after *Air Force One* landed at Washington's Andrews Air Force Base, Kennedy's body was transported by helicopter to Walter Reed Army Hospital and even produces transcripts of conversations occurring within *Air Force One* that the body would go to Walter Reed.

At Walter Reed Hospital, according to Lifton, a team of surgeons proceeded to alter the president's wounds. Lifton notes that two FBI agents, Francis X. O'Neill and James W. Sibert, assigned to guard the president's body during the autopsy at Bethesda, reported seeing not only the tracheotomy that Dallas doctors had performed on the president's throat but also "surgery of the head area, namely, in the top of the skull." No such surgery had been performed at Parkland Hospital. If there had been surgery it had occurred somewhere between Dallas and Bethesda, that is at Walter Reed.

Why would such surgery be performed? Lifton contends that the surgery altered JFK's wounds to erase evidence of bullets coming from the front and to create evidence of shots coming from the rear, the direction of the School Book Depository and Lee Harvey Oswald. It was, said Lifton, all part of a high-level plot to "introduce a false assassin," meaning Oswald.

Lifton, however, was unable to identify who would have been behind such a well-orchestrated conspiracy, beyond indicating that it had to include Secret Service personnel. He argued:

> The Secret Service furnished the bodyguards—controlled the trip planning, controlled the security at the moment of the shooting, controlled the speed of the car. The Secret Service had physical custody of the body, the clothing, the bullets, the limousine. The Secret Service had in its custody the X-rays and photographs taken at Bethesda. It would hardly be possible to implement the modus operandi described here without the involvement of some Secret Service personnel. And that is just the beginning. Others had to be involved.

6 Congress Fingers the Mob

By the mid-1970s the public's dissatisfaction with the Warren Report had reached a boiling point. In 1976 the U.S. House of Representatives responded and created the Select Committee on Assassinations (HSCA). The committee was charged with investigating both the John Kennedy and Martin Luther King killings, but most of its work focused on the JFK assassination.

The Fourth Shot

During the presidential motorcade, Dallas police officers and Secret Service agents kept in contact with each other over radio from their respective vehicles. Some of these conversations were recorded on tapes known as dictabelts. An assassination researcher named Gary Mack discovered these tapes and set to work to learn what was on them.

Mack paid particular attention to one tape, believed to have resulted from motorcycle policeman H. B. McLain's radio having gotten stuck in the on position during the assassination. Said Mack:

> I managed to get a tape of the police broadcasts and I worked on it. . . . There was some distortion because it was about a 13th generation tape . . . but it was then that I realized that the shots were in the tape . . . finding the precise location of the shots, then, was easy and (after filtering out much of the motorcycle engine noise) we heard the first shot . . . a very loud, sharp crack immediately following some conversation between two policemen.

If Mack's tape actually was recorded at Dealey Plaza during the shooting and if more than three shots could be found on it—or if acoustic analysis could prove that any shot originated from some-place other than the School Book Depository—the Warren Report would be proved wrong.

Mary Ferrell, a Dallas-based assassination researcher, brought the tapes to the HSCA, which engaged the acoustic analysis firm of Bolt, Beranek and Newman to run tests at Dealey Plaza to see if the results matched what was on the Dallas police dictabelt.

On Sunday morning, August 20, 1978, Bolt, Beranek and New-man performed a sound reconstruction. The streets around Dealey Plaza were closed off and sandbags were placed at four lo-cations on Elm Street to approximate the locations of the presi-dential vehicle as the shots were fired. Literally dozens of microphones were placed along Houston Street because that was the location of McLain's motorcycle when the assassination took place, but no one knew exactly where on the street. Then Bolt, Be-ranek and Newman arranged for shots to be fired from two loca-tions: from the School Book Depository's sixth floor and from atop the grassy knoll. Interestingly enough, the acoustics experts asked that the shots from the grassy knoll be fired with a pistol, even though almost no account of the assassination mentions that sort of weapon. In all fifty-six shots were fired, and the testing process went on all morning.

Motorcycle police ride alongside Kennedy's motorcade, unaware that the president has been shot. One of the police officers had kept his radio on, inadvertently recording the shots fired.

The results were inconclusive. About half the experts thought a second gunman was involved; the rest did not. The committee staff was almost ready to conclude that only one gunman, Oswald, was involved.

Again at the brink of confirming the Warren Report, the HSCA drew back for one last look. HSCA chief counsel G. Robert Blakey located two new acoustics experts, Professor Mark Weiss of the City University of New York and his research associate, Ernest Aschkenasy. They testified that the test results indicated that *four*, not three, shots had been fired at the president, and the third shot had not come from the depository but ". . . with a certainty factor of 95 percent or better, [was] fired at the Presidential limousine from the Grassy Knoll."

Jim Marrs wrote in *Crossfire:*

> Additionally, the tape showed that one shot came only 1.6 seconds behind another. Since the FBI had carefully determined that it required at least 2.3 seconds to fire the Mannlicher-Carcano rifle twice, this was further evidence of more than one assassin. Blakey shocked Committee members with this information.

Two gunmen meant a conspiracy to kill the president. Now the HSCA had to find out who was behind that conspiracy.

"The Motive, Opportunity and Means"

On November 22, 1963, G. Robert Blakey was a Justice Department attorney; Blakey's specialty was fighting organized crime. He had prosecuted such highly placed mob bosses as Santos Trafficante of Tampa, Florida, and Carlos Marcello of New Orleans. On the HSCA Blakey used his crime-fighting experiences to fashion a new assassination theory. The result was a final HSCA report contending that the mob had "the motive, opportunity and means" to murder President Kennedy.

Yet not all—or even most—elements of the syndicate were implicated. The "national syndicate of organized crime, as a group, were not involved in the assassination," the HSCA concluded, but it "could not preclude the possibility that individual members may have been involved."

Who were those individual mobsters?

The Umbrella Man

One of many shadowy figures of Dealey Plaza was the so-called umbrella man who had raised his black umbrella over his head, opened it, and then sat down on the curb as the shots were ringing out.

The Zapruder film had captured his movements, and many assassination researchers theorized he was signaling for the volley of rifle fire to begin. One theory even proposed that the umbrella referred to the umbrella of air cover promised the Cuban exiles at the ill-fated Bay of Pigs invasion and was meant to inform Kennedy of who would be responsible for his death.

Yet another researcher claimed the umbrella contained a poisoned flechette, or dart, that was shot into President Kennedy's throat. U.S. intelligence forces, it is alleged, developed such a weapon by 1963.

And standing next to the umbrella man was another mystery man, an Hispanic-looking individual, perhaps a Cuban, who seemed to be speaking into a walkie-talkie.

After the shooting stopped, neither followed the crowd up the grassy knoll; both walked off in separate directions.

The HSCA determined to find out who these two were and asked the public for assistance. Remarkably, the umbrella man himself came forward. He was Louis Steven Witt, a former insurance agent who said he had never been aware that his actions that day were so controversial. He had brought the umbrella to Dealey Plaza as a protest symbol to annoy the president. (Witt thought Kennedy had been appeasing foreign communists, and a black umbrella was the symbol of appeasement.) He still had the umbrella at his home and brought it to Washington to show the committee. He said he was slow to respond to the assassination because the umbrella had blocked his view of it.

The Hispanic-looking individual never came forward, but Witt said he wasn't Hispanic at all. He was black, never had a walkie-talkie, and sat on the curb, stunned and muttering to himself after the assassination.

Mobster Santo Trafficante allegedly said that President Kennedy was going to be killed by the mob for interfering in mob-run businesses.

"This Man Kennedy Is in Trouble"

Fidel Castro's seizure of power in Cuba in 1959 disturbed Americans for a number of reasons: the wave of refugees that fled his tyranny (eventually one-fifth of the entire country would leave), the seizure of hundreds of millions of dollars in U.S.-owned property, and the presence of Soviet advisers and missiles just ninety miles from the Florida coast. One factor, however, was particularly disturbing to the mob: Castro closed down numerous organized crime properties and enterprises.

Before 1959 Havana was a wide-open town, filled with lavish casinos, gambling, drugs, and vice. In charge of the mob's Havana operations was Tampa-born gangster Santos Trafficante. When Castro took over Cuba, he briefly jailed Trafficante. When the mob boss was released he cooperated in CIA efforts (unknown to President Kennedy) to assassinate the Cuban dictator.

In September 1963 Jose Aleman, a wealthy Cuban exile, met with Trafficante to discuss a $1.5 million Teamsters Union loan. When the conversation turned to the Kennedy brothers, Trafficante commented:

Have you seen how his brother is hitting [Teamsters president Jimmy] Hoffa [a corrupt union leader the Kennedy brothers had targeted for prosecution], a man who is a worker, who is not a millionaire, a friend of the blue collars? He doesn't know that this kind of encounter is very delicate. . . . It is not right what they are doing to Hoffa. . . . Hoffa is a hard-working man and does not deserve it. . . . Mark my words, this man Kennedy is in trouble and he will get what is coming to him.

Aleman boldly disagreed with the mobster, contending that Kennedy was a fine president who would easily be reelected. Trafficante responded, "You don't understand me. Kennedy's not going to make it to the election. He's going to be hit."

Aleman, an FBI informant, later insisted Trafficante "made it clear" he was not merely guessing about what would happen to Kennedy and also gave Aleman "the distinct impression that Hoffa was to be principally involved in the elimination of Kennedy." Aleman further claimed he promptly reported these conversations to

Jimmy Hoffa, Teamster president. Hoffa's connections to the mob made him a target for prosecution by the Kennedy brothers.

the FBI, but the FBI found nothing in its files to verify the assertion. When Aleman formally testified before the HSCA, his story changed significantly, and he said that maybe Trafficante had actually meant JFK would be "hit" by a flurry of Republican votes in the 1964 election. The HSCA doubted his story and found that "it is unlikely that Trafficante plotted to kill the President, although it could not rule out the possibility of such participation on the basis of available evidence."

Ominously, however, evidence emerged of a direct connection between Trafficante and Jack Ruby. A British journalist claimed that Ruby had met with Trafficante in 1959 in Trafficante's Havana jail cell. The story had the ring of credibility: Ruby had visited Cuba two or three times, once staying for a month. In August 1959 he visited the manager of the mob-controlled Tropicana Hotel for a week.

In March 1977 Trafficante took the Fifth Amendment (i.e., refused to testify on the grounds of self-incrimination) when ques-

Jack Ruby (pictured) was found to have connections with Santo Trafficante, the mobster. Could Ruby have killed Oswald to keep him quiet about the mob's connection to the assassination?

Jack Ruby

Was Jack Ruby a mob hit man ordered by his bosses to silence Lee Harvey Oswald?

The Warren Report concluded that there was not a "significant link between Ruby and organized crime," but many other researchers have noted his proven connections to gangsters and gamblers, particularly to Cuban-based Lewis McWillie. Ruby idolized McWillie, and it was on a trip to visit McWillie that Ruby allegedly met with mob boss Santos Trafficante.

Some have maintained that Ruby's seedy Dallas nightclub was involved in prostitution or drug trafficking or that he was involved in gunrunning to Cuba. In any case, Ruby had a history of violence. Part of his finger was bitten off in a brawl, and in 1953 he was arrested for attempted murder. "He liked to beat up drunks," wrote Seth Kantor in *Who Was Jack Ruby?*, "and more than once he would punch some woman hard enough to knock her down."

Jack Ruby passed a lie detector test when he told investigators "there was no conspiracy" to kill Oswald. But Ruby, whose mental state was deteriorating toward the end of his life and who tried to commit suicide several times, also informed television interviewers:

> Everything pertaining to what's happening has never come to the surface. The world will never know the true facts of what occurred, motives. . . . The people [who] had so much to gain and had such an ulterior motive to put me in the position I'm in will never let the true facts come above-board to the world.

tioned about what he told Aleman. When granted immunity, however, Trafficante admitted meeting with Aleman to discuss a Teamster loan but denied ever plotting JFK's assassination or ever meeting Ruby. Ruby himself took a polygraph and denied meeting Trafficante, and no other witnesses at the jail confirmed the original allegation.

Despite Trafficante's and Ruby's denials the HSCA found "there was considerable evidence" that a meeting between Ruby and Trafficante "did take place" and concluded that Ruby during his trips to Cuba "was most likely serving as a courier for gambling interests." Blakey went further, stating, "We came to believe that Ruby's trips to Cuba were, in fact, organized-crime activities."

"Take the Stone Out of My Shoe!"

New Orleans mob boss Carlos Marcello was another mobster who has been prominently linked to the JFK assassination. Considering Lee Harvey Oswald's New Orleans connections, Marcello was a particularly interesting name to emerge.

In 1963 oil-additive manufacturer Edward Becker and an associate, Carl Roppolo, met with Marcello at the mobster's three-thousand-acre plantation, Churchill Farms, just outside New Orleans. Becker recalls that at the mention of JFK's brother Bobby, Marcello became enraged and exclaimed in Italian, "Livarsi 'na pietra di la scarpa!" ("Take the stone out of my shoe!").

"Don't worry about that little Bobby son of a bitch," he screamed. "He's going to be taken care of." He talked about using a

Garrison and the Mob

Jim Garrison's flamboyant assassination probe investigated the CIA, Cuban exiles, and the New Orleans gay community, but there was one trail that his investigation never led to—organized crime. Where others would find connections between the Kennedy slaying and New Orleans mob boss Carlos Marcello, Garrison found none. He conspicuously ignored Ruby's underworld ties and Oswald's ties to Dutz Murret. Later researchers wondered why.

Life magazine reported that the mob-controlled Sands Hotel in Las Vegas had given Garrison a five-thousand-dollar line of credit. David Scheim in his *Contract on America* called one of Garrison's assistants, Pershing Gervais, "an admitted associate of Carlos Marcello" and pointed out that "Marcello bagman" Vic Carona had died of a heart attack at Garrison's home. Others called attention to Garrison's reputation for laying off Marcello-controlled gambling establishments.

"It is logical to ask," contended Scheim, "whether [Garrison's] probe was carried out with precisely [the] purpose . . . of deflecting attention from Carlos Marcello."

New Orleans mob boss Carlos Marcello. One witness claimed that Marcello had hinted that President Kennedy was going to be killed by the mob.

"nut" to carry out an assassination and added, "If you want to kill a dog, you don't cut off the tail, you cut off the head," meaning that instead of eliminating Robert Kennedy he would kill his brother the president. Becker claimed he didn't take Marcello's words seriously until after the assassination.

Researchers also discovered other links between the assassination and Marcello. Lee Harvey Oswald's uncle Dutz Murret was a small-time New Orleans gambler whom witnesses have associated with Marcello's crime organization. Some have suggested that it was Murret who brought his nephew to the attention of Mafia leaders who wanted a nut unconnected to them to perform their dirty work. Others have linked Oswald's mother, Marguerite Oswald, to a Marcello bodyguard.

Then there were connections between Marcello and Guy Banister and David Ferrie. Both did investigative work for Marcello's attorney, G. Wray Gill. During Ferrie's mysterious trip to Texas over the assassination weekend, he had made several calls back to Gill. When later questioned by the FBI, Ferrie was represented by Gill.

"He's Got to Go"

The committee also heard testimony from Louisiana Teamsters official Edward Partin.

The Brotherhood of Teamsters, one of the nation's largest and most powerful unions, had long been governed by shady practices and mob influence. Its leader, Jimmy Hoffa, hated both John and Robert Kennedy, but particularly the attorney general, who was an aggressive crime fighter.

In 1962 the union leader began to talk seriously to Partin about eliminating Bobby Kennedy ("I've got to do something about that son a bitch Bobby Kennedy. He's got to go.") and even asked him to secure a silencer for a gun and plastic explosives. Later Hoffa proposed that a lone gunman, not directly connected to the union, could assassinate Robert Kennedy using a rifle equipped with a telescopic sight.

The HSCA found that "Hoffa had believed that having the Attorney General murdered would be the most effective way of ending

President Kennedy confers with brother Robert. Could the mob have conspired to kill JFK to end Robert Kennedy's pressure on the mob's illegal activities?

the Federal Government's intensive investigation of the Teamsters and organized crime."

But Hoffa had plenty of venom for Jack Kennedy as well. Hoffa, said Partin, "hated Jack as much as Bobby" and would "fly off" whenever the president's name was mentioned.

The HSCA reported, "The Justice Department developed further evidence supporting Partin's disclosures, indicating that Hoffa had spoken about the possibility of assassinating the president's brother on more than one occasion."

"Jimmy Wants You to Kill the President"

Partin was not the last witness to link Hoffa and the mob to JFK's murder. In January 1992 former Teamsters attorney Frank Ragano told *New York Post* reporter Jack Newfield that in early 1963

> Jimmy [Hoffa] told me to tell Marcello and Trafficante they had to kill the President.

> I told them, "You won't believe what Hoffa wants me to tell you. Jimmy wants you to kill the President." They didn't laugh. They looked dead serious. They looked at each other in a way that made me uncomfortable. Their looks scared me. It made me think they already had such a thought in their mind.

After Kennedy's assassination Hoffa called Ragano, overjoyed about what he called the good news. Shortly thereafter five top Teamsters officials resigned, citing Hoffa's displeasure over their desire to send a simple condolence letter to the Kennedy family. Hoffa denied the story, but coldly issued a public statement saying that from now on Robert Kennedy would be "just another lawyer."

Sam Giancana

Jack Ruby and Lee Oswald are not the only two figures from that fateful weekend in Dallas to be linked by researchers to the mob. So has John F. Kennedy.

Although Jack Kennedy's brother Robert was pursuing a vigorous campaign against organized crime, rumors have long circulated that in 1960 JFK secured the presidency through mob support, both in terms of huge campaign contributions and vote fraud. According to mobster Mickey Cohen, "Certain people in

Chicago knew they had to get John Kennedy in. . . . John Kennedy was the best of the selection."

Kennedy's closest organized crime tie was to Chicago mob boss Sam Giancana. Judith Campbell, Giancana's girlfriend, was also a girlfriend of Kennedy's. Campbell has contended that she "was set up to be a courier" between the two powerful men and passed

Mob boss Sam Giancana (pictured) and JFK shared a common interest in Judith Campbell, who was girlfriend to both of them. Could Campbell have passed information between the two men?

Some conspiracy theorists believe that Judith Campbell acted as a courier between mobster Sam Giancana and JFK.

sealed envelopes to them at least ten times. She never opened the envelopes or learned what was in them.

In April 1962 FBI director J. Edgar Hoover let Kennedy know that he was aware of the JFK-Campbell-Giancana connection. The president quickly broke off the affair.

Just a month later, though, a shocked Kennedy learned that he had another connection to Giancana: The CIA informed him that it had hired Giancana and fellow mobster Johnny Roselli to help assassinate Fidel Castro.

"I trust that if you ever try to do business with organized crime again—with gangsters—" John Kennedy warned the CIA, "you will let the attorney general know."

Mobsters do not usually murder politicians or prosecutors. Why then would they murder Kennedy? Robert Blakey wrote in *The Plot to Kill the President*:

> You are all right, it is said, just as long as you do not "sleep with them," that is, you do not take favors, either money or sex. . . .

From the mob's point of view, Kennedy had been compromised. He had crossed the line. In the Greek [tragedy] sense, the liaison with Judith Campbell was, we came to believe, Kennedy's fatal flaw.

The HSCA report, based largely on new acoustic evidence of a second assassin, had stunned the nation with its finding that there was the "probability" of a conspiracy to kill JFK. It further concluded that there was the possibility of organized crime involvement in the plot. Robert Blakey had finally provided an official alternative to the Warren Commission Report.

In 1991 the Kennedy assassination and all the puzzling questions surrounding it were once again front-page news. That year Oscar-winning director Oliver Stone released the $40-million, star-studded film *JFK*, which raised questions about the Warren Report and focused on Jim Garrison's probe of Clay Shaw and the bizarre David Ferrie.

Director Oliver Stone during shooting for his film JFK. *Stone's film refueled several controversial conspiracy theories about the Kennedy assassination.*

"Why Aren't the Facts Enough?"

As a film *JFK* succeeded marvelously. Movie critic Roger Ebert called it "hypnotically watchable" and praised its "skillful interweaving of documentary footage." *USA Today*'s Mike Clark called it "a must-see for years."

But in subject matter Stone seemed to have gone too far. Out of all the conspiracy theories he could have recounted, he chose to support Jim Garrison's almost universally discredited investigation.

Stone, who had once called America "a fascist security state," also insinuated a massive conspiracy of high government officials to murder Kennedy. The result was a firestorm of hostile and even bitter criticism.

Time's Richard Corliss, who thought that cinematically *JFK* was a "knockout," called it "part history book, part comic book." Said John Connally: "At one time or another in the film, he involves the CIA, the FBI, the Secret Service, the military, the Warren Commission, President Johnson and the Mafia. This is ludicrous."

New York Times columnist Tom Wicker called *JFK* "paranoid and fantastic." Jack Valenti, head of the Motion Picture Association of

Oliver Stone re-creates the Kennedy assassination for his film JFK. *Stone's film, while celebrated as great cinema, was criticized for supporting several far-out conspiracy theories.*

America, condemned *JFK.* Valenti, a former aide to Lyndon Johnson, termed the film "a monstrous charade" and an "emotional diatribe." Mark Lane called it "bizarre." Comedian Mort Sahl, who in the 1960s had braved public condemnation to question the Warren Report, commented: "The real story is more interesting. Why aren't the facts enough?"

Yet Stone's controversial approach seized the public's imagination and hastened the release of the 848 cartons of HSCA files that had been locked away in the National Archives.

"Lee Had the Character to Kill Kennedy"

JFK's excesses seemed to set off a reaction against conspiratorial views of the assassination. Stone's almost all-encompassing conspiracy theory made many people deride the idea of such plots, and even though numerous conspiracy books continued to be published, in 1993 a major defense of the single-assassin theory emerged and reached national best-seller status. Gerald Posner's *Case Closed* combined old data, new scientific research, and material casting disturbing doubts on the reliability of key assassination-theory witnesses to fully support the Warren Report. The result was a new vigor in the traditionally one-sided debate on the question of who killed John F. Kennedy.

Posner examined such key issues as Jack Ruby's movements during the assassination weekend, Penn Jones's list of one hundred mysterious deaths, the magic-bullet theory, the reliability of grassy knoll witnesses, the HSCA's fourth shot, and possible mob involvement in JFK's slaying.

Also taking a new look at the assassination was novelist Norman Mailer, an early critic of the Warren Report. His 1995 book, *Oswald's Tale: An American Mystery*, is a psychological portrait of Lee Harvey Oswald. While unwilling to totally discard the idea of a second or other assassin, Mailer concludes, "Lee had the character to kill Kennedy and he probably did it alone. . . . Oswald—so far as he knew—was a lone gunman."

Oswald, Mailer believed, had thought that by killing Kennedy he would finally become known as one of the great men of history. At his trial Oswald could reveal ideas of a philosophy that towered over both capitalism and communism. But before that happened he panicked and shot police officer J. D. Tippit, an act that transformed him from a brave and valiant fighter for high ideals to a cheap cop-killer. "By killing Tippit," wrote Mailer, "he had wrecked his grand plan to be one of the oracles of history. Now he had to improvise a defense: I'm a patsy."

"They Pulled It Off"

Interviewed in the December 23, 1991, edition of *Time* magazine, filmmaker Oliver Stone explained the full implications of his film *JFK* and his vision of the widespread web of conspiracy surrounding the Kennedy assassination:

> I think the removal of the three most progressive leaders of the '60s [John and Robert Kennedy and Martin Luther King] during a time of bitterness and dissension and civil war in this country is very much tied into the assassination. I use the term civil war in its full implications, going back to the 1960s, where we were divided between hawks and doves, hippies and straights. These three leaders were pulling out of the war in Vietnam and shaking up the country. Civil rights, the cold war itself, everything was in question. There's no doubt that these three killings are linked, and it worked. That's what's amazing. They pulled it off. . . .
>
> As shown in the movie, the money that was involved was enormous by any standard. Cold war money. It's not just Vietnam money. It's military-industrial money. It's nuclear money. It's the American war economy that Eisenhower warned us about, that came into being in this country in the 1940s, after World War II. It's also the continuation of the covert state, the invisible government that operates in this country and seems to be an unelected parallel government to our legitimate government. The CIA and military intelligence all got out of hand somewhere in the 1960s. It suddenly reached another level, where the concept of assassination—the wet affair, liquidation—became the vogue.

Jack Ruby himself argued against having been part of a conspiracy theory, since his actions were almost completely random. "If it had been three seconds later I would have missed [Oswald]," he said.

"The Most Perfect Conspiracy in the History of the World"

A careful study of Jack Ruby's movements on the assassination weekend argues against his actions being part of a conspiracy or even that he himself had acted in any sort of coherent manner. On Friday night, Ruby gained entrance to the Dallas police headquarters and was present at Oswald's midnight press conference. He stood just a few feet away from Oswald and was armed. "Had I intended to kill him," he later told police, "I could have pulled my trigger on the spot, because the gun was in my pocket."

Ruby's itinerary on Sunday is crucial in determining what—if any—planning was involved in his actions. Even though Oswald's transfer to the county jail was scheduled for 10:00 A.M., Ruby slept late, probably not getting up until 9:00 at the earliest. At 10:19 he received a call from Little Lynn, a Carousel Club dancer who said she needed money. Ruby dressed slowly, and just before 11:00 A.M. he drove downtown (making an illegal U-turn in the process) to the Western Union office, just a single block from the police department, and wired her twenty-five dollars. As he approached Western Union he must have thought Oswald had already been transferred. There was a person ahead of him at the telegraph office, but Ruby didn't appear to be in any hurry. He did not use the pay phone at the building to signal anyone of his whereabouts or to receive any instructions. At exactly 11:17 A.M. the clerk gave him a receipt for the money order.

Meanwhile, Lee Harvey Oswald was still on the police station's third floor. Unexpectedly, Postal Inspector Harry D. Holmes showed up to interrogate Oswald about the post office box he had used to order his Mannlicher-Carcano rifle and his Smith and Wesson revolver. There was one last unexpected delay in moving the suspect that came from Oswald's request to put on his sweater before leaving the station. That delay would prove fatal.

At exactly 11:21 A.M.—nearly an hour and a half behind schedule—Oswald walked into the station's basement and was shot by Jack Ruby, who had seen the commotion at police headquarters and headed in to investigate. Ruby himself derided the idea of a plot and said his murder of Oswald had to be

> the most perfect conspiracy in the history of the world. . . . If it had been three seconds later I would have missed this person. . . . [H]ad I not made an illegal turn behind the bus to the parking lot, had I gone the way I was supposed to go, straight down Main Street, I would never had met this fate because the difference in meeting this fate was thirty seconds one way or the other.

The Grassy Knoll Witnesses

Posner and others analyzed the reliability of key witnesses who supported the grassy knoll theory.

Jesse Price, who told Mark Lane that he saw a man running from the grassy knoll with what "could have been a gun," was so hazy on what he saw that he said it might also have been a hat. He also thought he heard five shots and then a sixth "maybe as much as five minutes later." No such sequence of shots ever happened.

In his conclusion Posner writes:

> [The assassination researchers note] that "Price was never called to testify to the Warren Commission," implying that

The scene of JFK's assassination. The grassy knoll can be seen on the left, where some conspiracy theorists believe a second assassin was lying in wait.

the Commission wanted to avoid such a witness because it was not seeking the truth about what had happened at Dealey. Judging from Price's affidavit, the reason he was not called is obvious.

Sam Holland claimed he saw "a puff of smoke" rise from the grassy knoll. Posner notes that this elderly man was such a confused witness he thought Jacqueline Kennedy was trying to climb *into* the back seat after the shooting started and further that he had seen a Secret Service agent "with a machine gun" in the president's car. Neither event ever happened. When Holland reached the grassy knoll immediately after the shooting, he discovered nothing to indicate any shots had been fired. He even searched for spent shell casings on the ground but found none.

Lee Bowers Jr. was manning the fourteen-foot-high railroad control tower about fifty feet from the grassy knoll when the assassination took place. He told investigators he saw "a flash of light or smoke or something." Said Posner: "In order to perform any of his duties at the control board, Bowers would have had to have his

The Real Mr. X

In Oliver Stone's *JFK*, actor Donald Sutherland portrays an eerily friendly former intelligence officer who cryptically calls himself Mr. X and provides Jim Garrison with background on why an assassination would have occurred and who would have had the power to accomplish it.

Jim Garrison never actually met a Mr. X; that character is based on former air force colonel L. Fletcher Prouty, a one-time liaison to the CIA, who believes that Kennedy was killed by elements of the military-industrial complex because he was about to pull American forces out of Vietnam. "X exists," Stone once told a National Press Club audience. "He is sitting here on the podium. He is L. Fletcher Prouty."

Says Prouty:

> No one has to direct an assassination—it happens. The active role is secretly played by permitting it to happen. Kennedy was killed by the breakdown of the protective system that should have made an assassination impossible. . . . All the conspirators had to do was let the right "mechanics [assassins]" know.

back turned to Dealey Plaza." In regard to Bowers's claim of seeing smoke from a gun at the grassy knoll, Posner notes that modern ammunition is smokeless. Posner also reports that "when Oliver Stone filmed *JFK* he could not find a rifle that emitted enough smoke to be captured on film when fired from the grassy knoll. Finally, he resorted to a prop man pumping smoke from a bellows."

Author Jim Moore, an expert on the physical properties of Dealey Plaza, provided an explanation for what that smoke might actually have been. "I have, on several different occasions, noticed identical smoke there myself," he writes in *Conspiracy of One*. "It is generated by automobile exhaust when a car parked near the fence is started or idled."

Perhaps the most controversial witness cited by grassy knoll advocates, however, was Jean Hill, the lady in red. Her statements to investigators immediately following the assassination cast grave doubt on her credibility. She asserted that plainclothes officers fired back at the assassin and that Jackie Kennedy yelled out, "My

God, he has been shot!" Neither incident occurred. She also mistook the red roses laying on the car seat between the president and First Lady for a white dog.

Mrs. Hill could not have witnessed anyone suspicious running from behind the grassy knoll. Writes Moore:

> Standing where Mrs. Hill stood on November 22, you can't see behind the rise that culminates at the top of the knoll. It's impossible to see anyone running, walking, or standing behind the wooden fence, and you certainly can't observe anyone running toward the point where railroad tracks in the area join the triple underpass.

Moore also makes this final point about the grassy knoll issue:

> The critics don't want you to know that the grassy knoll afforded a would-be-assassin only a cross-shot—meaning the target moved across his field of vision from left to right rather than directly away, which is the more preferable of the two. Firing from atop the grassy knoll would hardly have been the choice of the discriminating assassin.

The Magic Bullet

Next to the grassy knoll, the so-called magic bullet has given assassination critics the most cause for concern. But recent scientific evidence has supported the Warren Commission's original single-bullet theory.

First, based on President Kennedy's and Governor Connally's wounds a research organization known as Failure Analysis Associates created a complex three-dimensional computer reconstruction of the assassination. The results: A single bullet caused all seven wounds, and it came from the sixth floor of the Book Depository.

As for the disputed weight of the famous stretcher bullet, Posner wrote: "All fragments from CE 399 weighed no more than 1.5 grains. That, added to the weight of CE 399 (158.6 [grams]) is still approximately 1 grain less than the weight of an average [Mannlicher-]Carcano bullet."

The HSCA had engaged Dr. Vincent Guinn to use neutron activation to determine if bullet fragments found in Kennedy and Connally matched CE 399. Neutron activation revealed that fragments from the stretcher bullet matched the fragments found in Connally's wrist. It also found a match between bullet fragments found in the president's skull and fragments found on the floor of the limousine's front seat. Said Dr. Guinn: "There is no evidence for three bullets, four bullets, or anything more than two."

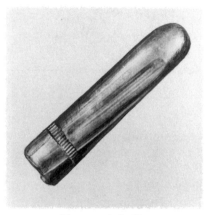

The magic bullet

Interestingly enough, neutron activation also proved that the bullet that came so close to killing General Edwin Walker was from the same brand of shells found on the sixth floor of the School Book Depository.

This new evidence once again pointed to a lone assassin. So did computer enhancement of the Zapruder film that found that the three shots had been fired not in 4.6 to 5.15 seconds as the Warren Commission had stated, but rather in 8.4 seconds, a time frame that more than allowed for Oswald to fire them.

The Fourth Shot

The cornerstone of the HSCA contention that a fourth shot had been fired rested largely on its analysis of the dictabelt. Without that evidence, the committee had little or no proof of a conspiracy. Tests by the National Science Foundation later disputed the HSCA's finding of four as opposed to three shots. The Committee on Ballistic Acoustics also found that "The acoustic analyses do not demonstrate that there was a Grassy Knoll shot . . . [and] do not support a conclusion that there was a second gunman."

Skeptics pointed to the absence of crowd noise or sirens from the dictabelt tape, indicating it was recorded somewhere besides Dealey Plaza. Instead, one can detect a bell softly tolling on the tape. There are no bells at Dealey Plaza. It has been suggested that the dictabelt sounds may have been originated at the Trade Mart, where a replica of the Liberty Bell was hung and was occasionally tapped by passersby.

Also, based on the detection of a voice heard on the tape (Dallas Sheriff Bill Decker saying, "Hold everything secure") the dictabelt could have been recorded as late as one minute after the actual assassination.

Jim Moore noted other reasons for doubting the HSCA's conclusions. Attacking what he called "lack of attention to detail" in the acoustic tests conducted at Dealey Plaza, he noted that the test shots were fired from an empty (as opposed to a carton-filled) sixth floor; there was no train on the triple overpass as there was on November 22, 1963; and two different types of ammunition were used. All circumstances would have provided different acoustic conditions.

Motorcycle policeman H. B. McLain also cast doubt on the HSCA findings. "That wasn't my motorcycle," he claimed on hearing the tape. "There would have been a siren on [my channel] all the way to the hospital. Everybody had their sirens on . . . you would have heard that." The HSCA had not allowed him to hear the dictabelt before he had testified that his microphone switch occasionally became stuck in the on position. "They knew that if I heard that tape I wouldn't testify for them," he revealed, "because I would immediately know that wasn't my cycle. If they wanted truthful answers they would have played the tape for me first."

Motorcycle policeman H. B. McLain claimed that the tape recording of the shooting could not have come from his motorcycle.

Gangsters

Skeptics also took new hard looks at the conclusion that mobsters may have been involved with the assassination.

Tampa organized crime boss Carlos Marcello had allegedly confided his desire to eliminate Kennedy to businessmen Edward Becker and Carl Roppollo, but HSCA investigators doubted that Marcello would share his thoughts on assassinating a president (or anyone for that matter) with so casual an acquaintance as Becker. They also found that he "had a questionable reputation for honesty and may not be a credible source of information." Also, Roppollo denied any such conversation had taken place.

Others questioned former Teamsters attorney Frank Ragano's contention that Jimmy Hoffa ordered Marcello and New Orleans mob boss Santos Trafficante to "hit" Kennedy. Steven Brill, author of *Teamsters*, countered that Ragano "was a peripheral figure. . . . Hoffa didn't order those guys [the mob] to do anything. They ordered Hoffa. . . . When he forgot he was their tool is when he got killed."

Others point out that Hoffa had once asked Marcello and Trafficante to kill his Teamsters rival Frank Fitzsimmons, but they refused, contending that Fitzsimmons was too important and they "could never touch him." If they were afraid to harm Fitzsimmons, how could they touch the president of the United States?

"The Critics Have Failed"

Summarized Gerald Posner:

> Time and technology have caught up with the conspiracy critics. Some of their most important contentions have collapsed; for example: Photographic tests reveal that the backyard photos of Oswald holding his weapons, contested as fakes, are authentic; ballistics and computer studies confirm the so-called magic bullet theory, long derided by conspiracy theorists as impossible; the neutron activation tests provide the final link that Oswald tried to assassinate General Edwin Walker, a crime for which many considered Oswald innocent. After thirty years of studying the case the critics have failed to produce a single, cogent, alternate scenario of how the conspiracy happened or who was involved.

Gangster Carlos Marcello is flanked by his attorneys. Investigators do not believe that Marcello would have been so open about his plans to assassinate Kennedy.

"Through the Looking Glass"

Despite the evidence presented by Posner, the debate over the assassination shows no signs of ending. New volumes continued to appear, opening new questions on the case, blaming everyone from the CIA to the Secret Service to Cuban exiles to the Dallas police to organized crime. Harold Weisberg, an early and persistent Warren Commission critic, even published *Case Open* to refute Posner.

It is likely that experts and members of the public alike will continue the heated debate about the circumstances surrounding John F. Kennedy's death. Said Jim Garrison, "The key to the whole case is through the looking glass. Black is white and white is black. I don't want to be cryptic, but that's the way it is."

Cast of Characters

Abt, John: Left-wing New York attorney requested by Lee Harvey Oswald.

Aleman, Jose: Miami-based Cuban exile; accused Florida mobster Santos Trafficante of saying JFK would be murdered before the 1964 presidential election.

Andrews, Dean: New Orleans attorney who triggered Jim Garrison's investigation of Clay Shaw; later convicted of perjury.

Aschkenasy, Ernest: Acoustics expert used by HSCA in establishing second gunman theory.

Baker, Marrion: Dallas motorcycle police officer; confronted Oswald within the School Book Depository but did not arrest him.

Banister, Guy: New Orleans private detective; former FBI agent; accused by Jim Garrison of plotting the assassination; died of a heart attack in 1964.

Bertrand, Clay: Alias supposedly used by Clay Shaw.

Bertrand, Clem: A variation on the Clay Bertrand alias supposedly used by Clay Shaw.

Bolt, Beranek and Newman: Acoustic analysis firm used by HSCA in establishing second gunman theory.

Bowers, Lee: Witness at Dealey Plaza; killed in 1966 in a highway accident.

Brennan, Howard: Key eyewitness against Lee Harvey Oswald.

Bundy, Vernon: Convicted heroin addict; witness against Clay Shaw.

Castro, Fidel: Cuban dictator; suspected by Lyndon Johnson of plotting JFK's murder.

Connally, John: Texas governor; former secretary of the navy; wounded in JFK assassination; later secretary of the treasury.

Connally, Nellie: Wife of John Connally; with Kennedy when he was assassinated.

Craig, Roger: Dallas County deputy sheriff who testified on behalf of Jim Garrison; later committed suicide.

Curry, Jesse: Dallas police chief.

Delgado, Nelson: Former marine; knew Oswald in marines and questioned his marksmanship abilities.

de Mohrenschildt, George: Texas oilman connected to CIA; mysterious friend of Lee Harvey Oswald; committed suicide in March 1977.

Ferrell, Mary: Dallas-based assassination researcher who brought dictabelt tape to HSCA's attention.

Ferrie, David: Airline pilot connected to anti-Castro Cubans and New Orleans mobsters; accused by Jim Garrison of plotting Kennedy's assassination.

Ford, Gerald: Warren Commission member; later U.S. president.

Garrison, Jim: New Orleans district attorney; unsuccessfully indicted Clay Shaw for assassination of John Kennedy.

Greer, Bill: Secret Service agent; drove the presidential limousine.

Hickey, George: Secret Service agent accused by Howard Donahue of accidentally killing Kennedy.

Hidell, A. J.: Alias used by Lee Harvey Oswald.

Hill, Clint: Secret Service agent; pushed Mrs. Kennedy back into the presidential limousine.

Hill, Jean: The so-called lady in red at Dealey Plaza.

Hoffa, Jimmy: Teamsters leader accused of plotting John and Robert Kennedy's assassination; mysteriously disappeared in July 1972; never found.

Holland, Sam: Witness at Dealey Plaza; saw a puff of smoke from grassy knoll.

Johnson, Lyndon Baines: John Kennedy's vice president; became president on JFK's death; believed Castro helped kill JFK; established Warren Commission.

Jones, Penn: Texas newspaper publisher and assassination theorist.

Kennedy, Jacqueline: Wife of John F. Kennedy.

Kennedy, John F.: President of the United States; assassinated in Dallas on November 22, 1963.

Kennedy, Robert: Brother of John F. Kennedy; attorney general of the United States; assassinated in 1968.

Lane, Mark: Pioneer conspiracy theorist; author of *Rush to Judgement*.

Lawson, Winston: Secret Service agent in charge of security for JFK's Dallas trip.

McLain, H. B.: Dallas motorcycle police officer whose microphone may have stuck on and resulted in the dictabelt tape used by the HSCA.

Mack, Gary: Assassination researcher key to the HSCA dictabelt tape investigation.

Marcello, Carlos: New Orleans mob boss suspected of ordering Kennedy's death; deported from United States by Robert Kennedy in 1961, returning shortly thereafter.

Martin, Jack: New Orleans private investigator; associate of Guy Banister and David Ferrie; original source of Jim Garrison's investigation into assassination.

Murret, Dutz: Uncle of Lee Harvey Oswald; resident of New Orleans.

Murret, Lillian: Aunt of Lee Harvey Oswald; resident of New Orleans.

Nosenko, Yuri: KGB defector who said the Soviets were not involved in the assassination.

O'Donnell, Kenneth: Aide to John F. Kennedy.

Oswald, Lee Harvey: Former marine; defector to Soviet Union; assassin of John F. Kennedy; murdered by Jack Ruby on November 24, 1963.

Oswald, Leon: Name given by Perry Russo as that of David Ferrie's roommate.

Oswald, Marina: Soviet-born wife of Lee Harvey Oswald.

Partin, Edward: Louisiana Teamsters official whom Jimmy Hoffa asked for help in killing Robert Kennedy.

Posner, Gerald: Author of *Case Closed*, an influential study of the assassination; argued only Oswald was involved in assassination.

Powers, Dave: Aide to John F. Kennedy; accompanied JFK's casket back to Washington.

Price, J. C.: Witness to the assassination; thought he saw a man running behind the grassy knoll; not called by Warren Commission.

Prouty, L. Fletcher: Conspiracy theorist; former air force intelligence officer; model for Mr. X character in Oliver Stone's *JFK*.

Ragano, Frank: Teamsters attorney who implicated Jimmy Hoffa in the JFK assassination.

Ruby, Jack: Dallas nightclub owner who murdered Lee Oswald on November 24, 1963.

Russo, Perry Raymond: Baton Rouge insurance salesman; Jim Garrison's key witness against Clay Shaw.

Shaw, Clay: New Orleans businessman accused by Jim Garrison of plotting John Kennedy's assassination; acquitted by New Orleans jury.

Spiesel, Charles: Highly unstable witness used by Jim Garrison against Clay Shaw.

Stone, Oliver: Oscar-winning filmmaker whose *JFK* rekindled the controversy over the assassination.

Tague, James T.: Witness at Dealey Plaza; injured by concrete fragment set loose by assassin's bullet.

Tippit, J. D.: Dallas police officer killed by Lee Harvey Oswald on November 22, 1963.

Trafficante, Santos: Florida mob boss; supposedly told Jose Aleman that Kennedy would be killed before the 1964 election.

Walker, General Edwin: Right-wing target of Lee Harvey Oswald's first assassination attempt.

Warren, Earl: U.S. Supreme Court chief justice; headed presidential commission (Warren Commission) to investigate assassination.

Witt, Louis: The so-called umbrella man at Dealey Plaza.

Yarborough, Ralph: U.S. senator; rival of John Connally.

Youngblood, Rufus: Secret Service agent responsible for guarding Lyndon Johnson.

Zapruder, Abraham: Dallas businessman who took most complete film of assassination.

For Further Reading

Lucy Post Frisbee, *John Fitzgerald Kennedy: America's Youngest President*. New York: Aladdin, 1986. A short biography of Kennedy, focusing on his youth but also touching on his presidency and death.

Susan Landsman, *Who Shot JFK?* New York: Avon Camelot, 1992. A brief but relatively balanced examination of the assassination.

Gene Schoor, *Young John Kennedy*. New York: Harcourt, Brace & World, 1963. A more detailed version of Lucy Frisbee's *John Fitzgerald Kennedy*. Ends with Kennedy's election to the presidency in 1960.

Jeffrey Waggoner, *The Assassination of President Kennedy*. Greenhaven Press: San Diego, 1989. Waggoner's book is a good summary of the most popular assassination theories. However, because it was written in 1989, it does not include material from recent works such as *Case Closed, Conspiracy of One,* and *Oswald's Tale* that cast doubt on many of the earlier theories.

Films

JFK. Directed, produced, and written by Oliver Stone and starring Kevin Costner with Tommy Lee Jones, John Candy, and Donald Sutherland. Stone's *JFK* may have started the reaction against conspiracy theories, but it gets high cinematic marks and won Oscars for best editing, best cinematography, and best supporting actor (Tommy Lee Jones as Clay Shaw), as well as nominations for best picture, best director, and best adapted screenplay. Look for Jim Garrison in the role of Earl Warren.

The Plot To Kill JFK. 98 min. MPI Home Video. This is actually a reissue of Mark Lane's 1966 documentary *Rush to Judgement* and a good overview of the early questions raised about the Warren Report. The film concentrates on disputing the Warren Commission Report and serves as a defense brief for Oswald.

Ruby. 110 min. Propaganda Films, 1992. Directed by John MacKenzie and starring Danny Aiello, Sherilyn Fenn, and Arliss Howard. If Jack Ruby was involved in a conspiracy, it certainly didn't happen this way. The character of Candy Cane, a dancer in Ruby's nightclub, is admittedly fictionalized. More for entertainment than actual analysis of Ruby's role in the assassination.

CD-ROM

JFK Assassination: A Visual Investigation. Richmond, VA: Medio Multimedia, 1993. A useful research tool containing the texts of the Warren Commission Report, Jim Marr's *Crossfire*, and *The Assassination of John F. Kennedy: The Complete Book of Facts.* Also includes animations of various theories, hundreds of photos, and several actual films (such as Abraham Zapruder's) of the assassination motorcade. The films can be viewed at regular speed, in slow motion, or even frame by frame.

Works Consulted

David W. Belin, *Final Disclosure: The Full Truth About the Assassination of President Kennedy*. New York: Charles Scribner's Sons, 1988. A brief volume that defends the findings of the Warren Commission by its former counsel.

Jim Bishop, *The Day Kennedy Was Shot*. New York: Funk & Wagnalls, 1968. Similar in scope to William Manchester's more famous *Death of a President*.

Mike Clark, "The Tampering and Temptations of 'JFK'," *USA Today*, December 20, 1991. A 3 1/2-star review of Oliver Stone's *JFK*.

Richard Corliss, "Who Killed J.F.K.?" *Time*, December 23, 1991. An analysis of the controversy surrounding Oliver Stone's *JFK*.

James P. Duffy and Vincent L. Ricci, *The Assassination of John F. Kennedy: A Complete Book of Facts*. New York: Thunder's Mouth Press, 1992. Not as complete as the title suggests. Faithfully reports allegations, but often fails to relate any contradictory data.

Edward Jay Epstein, *Legend: The Secret World of Lee Harvey Oswald*. New York: McGraw-Hill, 1978. A look at Oswald's activities leading up to and including his defection to the Soviet Union. Unlike many other books that present an alternate view of Oswald and the assassination, *Legend* takes a reasoned and plausible approach to the subject.

Jim Garrison, *On the Trail of the Assassins*. New York: Warner Books, 1988. Jim Garrison's story told in an almost detective-novel fashion.

Robert J. Groden and Harrison Edward Livingstone, *High Treason*. New York: Berkley Books, 1990. A not-very-convincing attempt to tie the assassination to just about everyone.

Henry Hurt, *Reasonable Doubt: An Investigation into the Assassination of John F. Kennedy*. New York: Holt, Rinehart & Winston, 1985. One of the more organized and plausible criticisms of the Warren Report.

Seth Kantor, *Who Was Jack Ruby?* New York: Everest House, 1978. Kantor believes Ruby acted on mob orders with Dallas police assistance. Very interesting details on Ruby not found in other assassination books.

Janet M. Knight, *Three Assassinations: The Deaths of John and Robert Kennedy and Martin Luther King.* New York: Facts On File, 1971. An excellent no-nonsense source of material not only on the JFK and Oswald shootings but also on the Garrison probe.

David Landis, "Guv Pans JFK Pic," *USA Today*, December 24, 1991. John Connally's comments on *JFK.*

David Landis, "Valenti's JFK Retort," *USA Today*, April 3, 1992. Jack Valenti's comments on *JFK.*

Mark Lane, *Plausible Denial: Was the CIA Involved in the Assassination of JFK?* New York: Thunder's Mouth Press, 1992. In this book, Lane details allegations regarding the involvement of Watergate conspirator E. Howard Hunt and the CIA in the assassination and even gently hints that George Bush may have been involved. Marred by Lane's egotistical style of writing.

Mark Lane, *Rush to Judgement.* New York: Thunder's Mouth Press, 1992. Without question the most influential volume to cast doubt on the Warren Report. This updated edition also contains Lane's analysis of *JFK.*

David S. Lifton, *Best Evidence: Disguise and Deception in the Assassination of John F. Kennedy.* New York: Carroll & Graf, 1988. Lifton's main theory is that Kennedy's wounds were surgically altered to cover up evidence that Kennedy was shot from the front. He also believes that Kennedy's body was removed from its coffin while on board *Air Force One.*

Norman Mailer, *Oswald's Tale: An American Mystery.* New York: Random House, 1995. A biography of Oswald with heavy emphasis—and much original research—on his stay in the Soviet Union.

Priscilla Johnson McMillan, *Marina and Lee.* New York: Bantam Books, 1978. Written with the assistance of Marina Oswald, this is one of the most complete and valuable portraits of Lee Harvey Oswald that we have.

William Manchester, *The Death of a President.* New York: Harper & Row, 1967. The Kennedy family authorized this exhaustive study of the assassination weekend.

Bonar Menninger, *Mortal Error: The Shot That Killed JFK.* New York: St. Martin's Press, 1992. A revisionist history that is not a conspiracy theory. The author contends that a Secret Service agent actually fired the shot that killed President Kennedy.

Jim Moore, *Conspiracy of One: The Definitive Book on the Kennedy Assassination.* Fort Worth: The Summit Group, 1991. The author is an expert on the assassination site, and makes a good (but emotional) case against the many conspiracy theories. Not nearly as compelling as *Case Closed*, but still valuable. Moore's theory on the first shot is not new; Jim Bishop stated it first in *The Day Kennedy Was Shot.*

Gerald Posner, *Case Closed: Lee Harvey Oswald and the Assassination of JFK.* New York: Anchor Books, 1993. A compelling demolition of the Warren Report's critics, but most interesting are the very human—but pathetic—portraits of Oswald and Ruby. Although this edition contains material not found in the first edition, it still does not answer all of the questions raised by the dozens of alternate views of the JFK assassination.

The President's Commission on the Assassination of President Kennedy, The Warren Commission Report. New York: Barnes & Noble Books, 1992. Although derided by numerous critics, this is the *one* book from which all discussion of the assassination starts. For all its faults, the report contains an incredible wealth of information.

David E. Scheim, *Contract on America: The Mafia Murder of President John F. Kennedy.* New York: Zebra Books, 1989. Scheim's book goes beyond linking the mob to JFK's murder and spins out a complex theory of organized crime's influence within the highest levels of U.S. government that stretches over several decades. Heavily footnoted.

Tom Squitieri, "JFK Files May Shed Light on Witness's Death," *USA Today*, March 20, 1992. Information on George de Mohrenschildt.

Tom Squitieri, "What's in Files," *USA Today*, March 20, 1992. Additional information on George de Mohrenschildt.

Time, "Died, Major General Edwin A. Walker," November 15, 1993. Obituary of Oswald's first target.

USA Today, "He's No Fan of 'JFK' Film," December 20, 1991. Comedian and social critic Mort Sahl's comments on *JFK*.

Index

Picture Credits

About the Author

David Pietrusza has written for numerous publications including *Modern Age, The Journal of Social and Political Studies, Academic Reviewer,* and *The New Oxford Review.* For two years he produced the nationally syndicated radio program *National Perspectives.* His *The End of the Cold War, The Invasion of Normandy, The Battle of Waterloo,* and *The Chinese Cultural Revolution* have also been published by Lucent.

Pietrusza has also written extensively on the subject of baseball. He is president of the Society for American Baseball Research (SABR) and managing editor of *Total Baseball IV,* the official encyclopedia of Major League Baseball. His three books on baseball are *Minor Miracles, Major Leagues,* and *Baseball's Canadian-American League.* In 1994 Pietrusza served as a consultant for PBS's Learning Link online system and produced the documentary *Local Heroes* for PBS affiliate WMHT.

He lives with his wife, Patricia, in Scotia, New York.